CAMPAIGN 274

SHENANDOAH 1864

Sheridan's valley campaign

MARK LARDAS

ILLUSTRATED BY ADAM HOOK
Series editor Marcus Cowper

First published in Great Britain in 2014 by Osprey Publishing,
PO Box 883, Oxford, OX1 9PL, UK
PO Box 3985, New York, NY 10185-3985, USA

E-mail: info@ospreypublishing.com
© 2014 Osprey Publishing Ltd

OSPREY PUBLISHING IS PART OF THE OSPREY GROUP.

A CIP catalog record for this book is available from the British Library.

ISBN: 978 1 4728 0483 9
E-book ISBN: 978 1 4728 0507 2
ePub ISBN: 978 1 4728 0508 9

Editorial by Ilios Publishing Ltd, Oxford, UK (www.iliospublishing.com) and Nikolai Bogdanovic
Index by Zoe Ross
Typeset in Myriad Pro and Sabon
Maps by Bounford.com
3D bird's-eye views by The Black Spot
Battlescene illustrations by Adam Hook
Originated by PDQ Media, Bungay, UK
Printed in China through Worldprint Ltd.

14 15 16 17 18 10 9 8 7 6 5 4 3 2 1

ARTIST'S NOTE

Readers may care to note that the original paintings from which the color plates in this book were prepared are available for private sale. The Publishers retain all reproduction copyright whatsoever. The artist can be contacted at the following address:
Scorpio, 158 Mill Road, Hailsham, East Sussex BN27 2SH, UK
Email: scorpiopaintings@btinternet.com
The Publishers regret that they can enter into no correspondence upon this matter.

THE WOODLAND TRUST

Osprey Publishing are supporting the Woodland Trust, the UK's leading woodland conservation charity, by funding the dedication of trees.

IMAGE CREDITS

The following abbreviations indicate the sources of the illustrations used in this volume:
LOC   Library of Congress, Washington DC
AC   Author's collection

AUTHOR'S DEDICATION

This book is dedicated to my son Benjamin, the Eagle in the family.

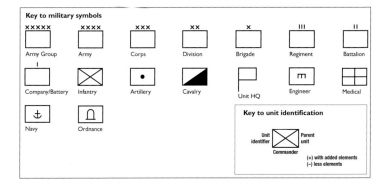

CONTENTS

ORIGINS OF THE CAMPAIGN

The Union and the Confederacy battled over the Shenandoah Valley of Virginia for three years. Nestled between the Blue Ridge Mountains to the east and the Valley and Ridge Appalachians to the west, the valley served as granary for General Robert E. Lee's Army of Northern Virginia, providing bread and beef to feed this shield of the Confederacy, and fodder and remounts for its cavalry. The reinforcements that turned the tide at the First Battle of Bull Run (or First Manassas) on July 21, 1861 and yielded a Confederate victory came from the Shenandoah. In addition, the Shenandoah formed a sheltered highway to the north for the forces of the Confederacy during their invasion of Maryland in 1862 and Pennsylvania in 1863.

The Union tried to wrest control of the valley from the Confederacy in 1862. Its forces took the northern half of the valley, even beating the Confederates commanded by the vaunted Thomas "Stonewall" Jackson at the First Battle of Kernstown on March 23. Jackson then outhustled three Union armies and ignominiously chased them from the Shenandoah. His infantry moved so quickly that thereafter they were called "Jackson's Foot Cavalry."

The Union was so badly beaten they all but left the Shenandoah alone in 1863. In 1864 the United States Army's new general-in-chief, Ulysses S. Grant, created the Union's first cohesive strategy for conquering the Confederacy. Its primary goal was the destruction of the Confederate field armies. Geographic objectives only existed to the extent that they supported this mission. The Shenandoah's role in feeding Lee's forces reinstituted its strategic importance for the Union; taking the valley would starve the Army of Northern Virginia into submission. Two Union armies advanced into the Shenandoah in the spring of 1864: one came over the Appalachians from West Virginia, while the second marched from the mouth of the Shenandoah river at Harpers Ferry.

Grant's initial plans came a cropper. In early July 1864 Lee sent a corps under the command of Lieutenant-General Jubal Early to counter the Union invasion of the Shenandoah Valley. In a brilliant six-week campaign, Early first drove Union forces out of the valley, and then launched the last Confederate invasion of the Union states, moving his independent command into Maryland and marching to the gates of Washington DC.

Although the raid caused panic in Washington, Early lacked the forces to overcome the determined defense and capture the capital. Moroever, few in the North realized how weak Early's forces really were. Jubal Early continued his game of hitting the North at unexpected spots. He marched into Pennsylvania and burned Chambersburg in late July 1864. Before the North could react, he returned to the Shenandoah Valley.

Grant was forced to transfer a corps from the Army of the Potomac, then besieging Petersburg, Virginia to the District of Columbia. He was unhappy about the loss of troops, the failure to control the Shenandoah and particularly about Early's ability to raid the North with impunity. Grant created a new command on August 1, 1864, adding the reinforcements sent to the Union forces in Washington (who had previously been chased out of the Shenandoah) to form the Union Army of the Shenandoah.

Grant realized that defeating Early was less a matter of troops than of leadership. The Union commanders that had already clashed with Early in the Shenandoah Valley—Franz Sigel and David Hunter—had both had sufficient numbers of men to defeat him. However, both lacked the necessary military and leadership skills required for victory. Grant needed someone capable of taking charge of the resources already in the vicinity of the Shenandoah and of achieving the right results.

After chasing Major-General Franz Sigel's and Major-General David Hunter's army out of the Shenandoah in the opening phase of the Valley Campaigns of 1864, Early took his independent command known as the Army of the Valley into Maryland, threatening Washington DC. His army turned back after reaching Fort Stevens, on the capital's outskirts. (AC)

At first Grant considered giving Major-General George Meade the assignment. However, reassigning Meade from his command of the Army of the Potomac was viewed as an undeserved demotion by Lincoln and other senior army officials. As a result, Grant decided against this. Instead, after considering several other candidates, Grant selected the cavalry commander Brigadier-General Philip Henry Sheridan.

Following the Washington raid, Early marched into Pennsylvania to collect food and fodder for his army. During the sweep, the raiders burned the town of Chambersburg in late July 1864 in retaliation for Hunter's burning of the Virginia Military Institute in Lexington, Virginia in June. (AC)

It was a surprising choice. Sheridan, a 5ft 4in. bantam of a man, was a first-lieutenant in March 1861. Battlefield competence led to a meteoric rise from captain to major-general over a six-month period between 1862 and 1863 (with promotion to major-general in the regular army following in October 1864). Grant now wanted Sheridan take command of an army, putting Sheridan, then just 33 years old, on nearly the same level as William T. Sherman and George Meade.

Despite objections, Grant prevailed. Sheridan was sent to Harpers Ferry to take command of VI Corps (detached from the Army of the Potomac when Early raided Washington), two divisions of XIX Corps (reassigned from the Mississippi), and the corps-sized Army of West Virginia. Grant's instructions to Sheridan were, simply, "to put himself south of the enemy, and follow him to the death. Wherever the enemy goes, let our troops go also. Once started up the Valley they ought to be followed until we get possession of the Virginia Central Railroad."

On August 7, 1864 Sheridan assumed command of the Army of the Shenandoah. Over the next 90 days two armies—the Union forces led by Philip Sheridan and the Confederate troops commanded by Jubal Early—would maneuver across the Shenandoah Valley. It would be a campaign of move and countermove, where unexpected attacks would be met by equally unexpected ripostes. In a series of changing fortunes, victory would turn into defeat, to be followed once again by victory.

The stakes were far higher than the fate of a disputed agricultural valley. The consequences of the campaign would be felt throughout a nation torn apart by civil war. Victory or defeat in the Shenandoah Valley would affect the outcome of the presidential election to be held in November 1864. It would affect the strength of the Confederate armies throughout the Confederacy. A Confederate loss of the valley would cripple the Army of Northern Virginia, which drew critical supplies from the area.

The outcome of the campaign, perhaps more than any other in the Civil War, rested on the shoulders of one man—the commander of the Union Army of the Shenandoah, viewed by many on both sides as too inexperienced for the job. His impact was so marked, however, that afterwards, despite almost equally impressive efforts by his opposite number, the events would become known as "Sheridan's Valley Campaign."

The Shenandoah Valley campaigns, August–October 1864.

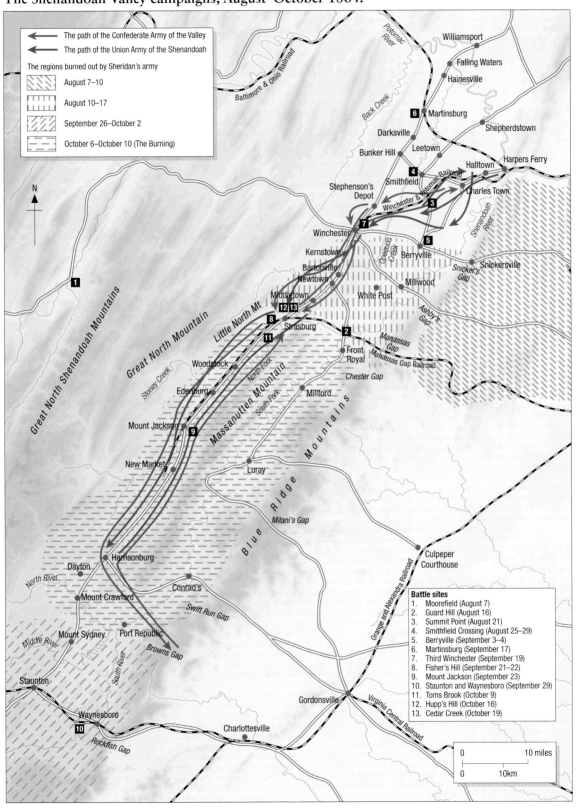

The path of the Confederate Army of the Valley
The path of the Union Army of the Shenandoah

The regions burned out by Sheridan's army

August 7–10

August 10–17

September 26–October 2

October 6–October 10 (The Burning)

N

Battle sites
1. Moorefield (August 7)
2. Guard Hill (August 16)
3. Summit Point (August 21)
4. Smithfield Crossing (August 25–29)
5. Berryville (September 3–4)
6. Martinsburg (September 17)
7. Third Winchester (September 19)
8. Fisher's Hill (September 21–22)
9. Mount Jackson (September 23)
10. Staunton and Waynesboro (September 29)
11. Toms Brook (October 9)
12. Hupp's Hill (October 16)
13. Cedar Creek (October 19)

0   10 miles
0   10km

Potomac River
Williamsport
Falling Waters
Hainesville
Baltimore & Ohio Railroad
Back Creek
6 Martinsburg
Shepherdstown
Darksville
Leetown
Bunker Hill
Halltown
Harpers Ferry
Stephenson's Depot
Smithfield
4
Charles Town
Winchester & Potomac Railroad
3
7
Shenandoah River
Winchester
5
Kernstown
Berryville
Snickersville
Opequon Creek
Bartonville
Snicker's Gap
Newtown
Millwood
White Post
Middletown
12 13
Ashby's Gap
8
Little North Mt
Strasburg
2
11
Front Royal
Manassas Gap
Stoney Creek
Woodstock
North Fork
Manassas Gap Railroad
Great North Mountain
Edenburg
Chester Gap
Millford
South Fork
Great North Shenandoah Mountains
Mount Jackson
9
New Market
Luray
Massanutten Mountain
Milani's Gap
Blue Ridge Mountains
Culpeper Courthouse
Orange and Alexandra Railroad
Harrisonburg
Dayton
North River
Conrad's
Swift Run Gap
Mount Crawford
Mount Sydney
Port Republic
Middle River
Browns Gap
South River
Staunton
Gordonsville
Virginia Central Railroad
Waynesboro
10
Charlottesville
Rockfish Gap

1

CHRONOLOGY

1864

June 12	Early's Corps (II Corps, Army of Northern Virginia) is ordered to the Shenandoah to reinforce Confederate forces there.
June 17–18	Battle of Lynchburg.
June 20	Union Major-General Hunter evacuates the Shenandoah Valley.
July 5	Early invades Maryland.
July 9	Battle of Monocacy.
July 11–12	Battle of Fort Stevens, on the outskirts of Washington DC.
July 14	Early withdraws to the Shenandoah Valley.
July 30	Confederate cavalry raid takes place in Pennsylvania. Chambersburg is burned.
August 6	Sheridan takes command of Middle Military Division (also known as the Army of the Shenandoah).
August 7	Battle takes place at Moorefield, West Virginia.
August 10	Early abandons Bunker Hill, West Virginia, falling back to Fisher's Hill. Union cavalry sweeps into the Shenandoah Valley and Loudoun County. Wheat and hay are destroyed and cattle are driven off between Winchester and Berryville.
August 11	Cavalry skirmishing takes place at Double Toll Gate.
August 16	Battle of Guard Hill.
August 17	Early advances north from Fisher's Hill, and catches Sheridan's rearguard at Abrams Creek.

August 21	Battle of Summit Point.
August 25–29	Battle of Smithfield Crossing.
August 31	Kershaw's Division, Cutshaw's Artillery, and I Corps commander Richard Anderson are ordered back to Petersburg by Early.
September 2	Sherman captures Atlanta.
September 3–4	Kershaw's troops encounter Union forces at Berryville while marching out of the Shenandoah. The Battle of Berryville results.
September 14	Kershaw's Division, Cutshaw's Artillery, and Richard Anderson once again leave Early's army to return to Lee, marching further south to avoid Union troops at Berryville.
September 17	Early attacks Brigadier-General William W. Averell at Martinsburg, leaving Winchester lightly held.
September 19	Third Battle of Winchester (or Opequon) takes place.
September 20	Early reoccupies Fisher's Hill entrenchments.
September 21–22	Battle of Fisher's Hill takes place.
September 23	Skirmish at Mount Jackson. Early departs before Sheridan's main body arrives.

The Third Battle of Winchester (or Opequon, as Sheridan preferred) took place on September 19 and was the first major battle of Sheridan's campaign. The VI Corps used Sprout's Spring Mill, shown here, as a hospital during the battle. (AC)

September 24	Early retreats from Rude's Hill to Port Republic.
September 25	Sheridan's infantry occupies Harrisonburg.
September 26	Early reaches Browns Gap, and is joined by Kershaw's Division and the cavalry covering the Luray Valley.
September 29	Brigadier-General Alfred Torbert's cavalry raids Staunton and Waynesboro. Systematic confiscation or destruction of barns, mills, and livestock between Staunton and Mount Crawford begins.
October 2	Destruction of the area between Staunton and Mount Crawford is complete.
October 3	Sheridan decides to abandon the upper valley, and devastates the area between Mount Crawford and Harrisonburg.
October 5	Early leaves Browns Gap to attack Sheridan at Harrisonburg.
October 6	Sheridan departs Harrisonburg.
October 6–10	"The Burning"—the systematic confiscation or destruction of barns, mills, crops, and livestock between Harrisonburg and Strasburg, across the width of the valley.

The Battle of Cedar Creek on October 19 was the largest, most decisive and final battle of Sheridan's Shenandoah campaign. It opened with a Confederate attack, but ended with the Union cavalry sweeping the Confederates off the field. (AC)

October 9	Battle of Toms Brook.
October 10	Sheridan reaches his new permanent encampment at Cedar Creek, north of Strasburg.
October 13	Early reoccupies Fisher's Hill.
October 15	Sheridan is ordered to meet with Secretary of War Edwin M. Stanton in Washington DC.
October 16	Battle of Hupp's Hill.
October 17	Sheridan meets with Stanton in Washington DC, and then leaves for Martinsburg.
October 18	Sheridan arrives at Winchester. Confederate Major-General John B. Gordon begins marching his men over Massanutten Mountain to attack the Union encampments at Cedar Creek.
October 19	Battle of Cedar Creek.
November–December	Both armies enter winter quarters.

1865

February	Sheridan resumes his offensive.
March 2	The Battle of Waynesboro—Early's final battle.
March 29–April 9	The Appomattox campaign takes place, culminating in Lee's surrender.
June 10	General Edmund Kirby Smith's Confederate army surrenders—the last to do so—bringing the Civil War to an end.

OPPOSING COMMANDERS

By the fall of 1864 the military leadership of both armies—Union and Confederate—achieved a competence for which Abraham Lincoln and Jefferson Davis would have hungered in 1861. The outright incompetent were gone, having been exposed and weeded out. Merely competent commanders had largely been shifted to secondary theaters, or placed in positions that required little brilliance. There would be leadership failures in 1864 and 1865—including spectacular ones on both sides—but these were usually the result of otherwise good leaders being placed in commands beyond their leadership abilities or in positions outside their core competencies.

Moreover, the war served as a sifter, shaking out the dross, and bringing to the fore the very best leaders. Men who spent the pre-war decades without rising above lieutenant or captain rocketed into high command due to superior performance on the battlefield. No theater of war better illustrated this dynamic than the Shenandoah Valley in 1864. It started the year as a secondary theater. The officers commanding, on both sides, were adequate, but not spectacular. The strategic importance of the valley forced Lee to reinforce it once Grant launched an offensive there. Lee attempted to make up for a lack of manpower with superior leadership, sending the best officers he had. That leadership allowed the Confederacy to reverse the earlier Union advances and move to the offensive. In turn, their actions led Grant to replace his generals with the best he had available. The result was a campaign featuring the best against the best. Superior leadership was the baseline requirement; merely average leadership would court disaster.

Lincoln described Phil Sheridan as "A brown, chunky little chap, with a long body, short legs, not enough neck to hang him, and such long arms that if his ankles itch he can scratch them without stooping." The trademark pork-pie hat Sheridan wore was one of the few types that fitted him. (LOC)

UNION COMMANDERS

Brigadier-General Philip H. Sheridan
Phil Sheridan was born March 6, 1831 to Irish immigrant parents. Where he was born is obscure. He claimed to have been born in Albany, New York although others claim he had been born in

his parents' homeland in County Cavan, Ireland or Somerset, Ohio where he spent his childhood. Regardless, he was a man of Ohio, receiving his appointment to the United States Military Academy at West Point from Ohio Congressman Thomas Ritchey, who represented Somerset in the House of Representatives. He graduated in 1853, a year late, after being suspended for a year for fighting. He was 34th in his class of 52 cadets.

Between receiving his commission as a second lieutenant in the infantry in 1853 and the start of the American Civil War, Sheridan served in the 1st Infantry in Texas and the 4th Infantry in the Pacific Northwest. At the Civil War's outset, Sheridan was still a second lieutenant. He was promoted to captain after the Battle of Fort Sumter in April 1861.

Ordered to Missouri, upon arrival he experienced a meteoric career rise. He was promoted to colonel and given command of the 2nd Michigan Volunteer Cavalry in May 1862, then to brigadier-general and command of an infantry division in September (the promotion was backdated to July 1). He fought at Perryville, Stones River, Chickamauga, and Chattanooga, performing well. His division was one of two that broke the Confederate center at Chattanooga.

When Grant became General-in-Chief of the Armies of the United States in 1864 and relocated his headquarters to the Army of the Potomac, he brought Sheridan with him. Although Sheridan was an infantry officer, Grant gave Sheridan command of the Cavalry Corps, believing that "Little Phil's" aggressiveness would give the Army of the Potomac's cavalry the initiative it long lacked.

Sheridan succeeded in firing up his command. The Cavalry Corps was detached from the Army of the Potomac and attached to the Army of the James to conduct a raid on Richmond in May 1864. While Sheridan's raid resulted in the death of J.E.B. Stuart at the Battle of Yellow Tavern, critics noted his cavalry had little strategic effect on Grant's 1864 Overland Campaign. Despite that, Grant saw something in his young subordinate others did not. Grant appointed Sheridan overall commander of the new and unified Union military district in the Shenandoah.

Major-General Horatio G. Wright

Commander of the Union VI Corps, Horatio Wright was born March 6, 1820. He attended West Point, graduating second in his class of 52 in 1841, and received a commission in the Engineers. A career soldier, prior to the Civil War he taught engineering at West Point, and oversaw construction of coastal fortifications. During the Civil War he served in a variety of roles, gaining command of the 1st Division of VI Corps in May 1863. He took command of the corps following the death of its commander, General John Sedgwick, at the Battle of the Wilderness in May 1864.

Peppery and competent, Horatio Wright commanded VI Corps during Sheridan's campaign in the Shenandoah. He made few mistakes on the battlefield, but his decision to bring his baggage train along at the Third Battle of Winchester almost cost the Union victory. (LOC)

He was a competent but not brilliant commander. Although he made errors that cost one Union victory early in the campaign, he was slow to panic and steady in battle—traits that proved invaluable. His VI Corps would be the only Union corps never routed during the Shenandoah campaign.

Brigadier-General William H. Emory

Born and raised in Maryland, William H. Emory attended West Point, graduating 14th in a class of 33 in 1831. He received a commission in the artillery, but spent most of his ante-bellum military career as a topographic engineer. Despite his Southern heritage and although offered a major-general's commission in the Confederate Army, Emory remained loyal to the national government. Initially serving in the Army of the Potomac, Emory went to Louisiana, where he rose to command XIX Corps. He commanded XIX Corps during the Shenandoah campaign. Along with Horatio Wright, Emory provided competent leadership, keeping his troops steady in adverse conditions.

Brigadier-General George Crook

George Crook commanded the corps-sized Army of West Virginia during Sheridan's Valley Campaign. As with the other corps commanders, Crook

Alfred Torbert commanded the Army of the Shenandoah's Cavalry Corps during the campaign. Sheridan was never fully satisfied with Torbert's performance. When Sheridan left the Shenandoah in April 1865, he turned over the remnants of the Army of the Shenandoah to Torbert, and gave Torbert's Cavalry Corps to Wesley Merritt. (AC)

attended West Point, graduating in 1852 near the bottom of his class—38th out of 43. Following graduation, he served in the 4th Infantry in the Pacific Northwest. He served with Philip Sheridan, and they became friends. His initial Civil War command was that of a regiment in Western Virginia. His unit transferred to the Army of the Potomac with General John Pope. Crook fought at Second Bull Run and Antietam. He moved back to Western Virginia to take command of the Kanawha Division. Over the next year he was transferred to a number of different commands in the Department of the Ohio and Army of the Cumberland, before returning to command the Kanawha Division in the spring of 1864.

During the Union assaults on the Shenandoah in the spring and summer of 1864, Crook led one of the Union columns attacking the valley. Despite being repulsed at the Second Battle of Kernstown in July 1864, he was retained as commander of the Army of West Virginia, replacing Major-General David Hunter as its field commander.

Major-General Alfred T.A. Torbert

Torbert commanded the Cavalry Corps of the Army of the Shenandoah during Sheridan's Valley Campaign. Born in Delaware, he attended West Point, graduating 21st in a class of 34 in 1855. Commissioned in the infantry, prior to the Civil War he served in various postings in the American West in the 2nd Infantry. Offered a Confederate commission at the start of the war, he refused it, instead accepting a commission in a New Jersey regiment. He served in the Army of the Potomac, seeing action in most of the major battles fought by that army, from the Second Battle of Bull Run (or Second Manassas) in late August 1862 through the Overland Campaign of 1864. Given command of the 1st Cavalry Division in that army in April 1864, Torbert was senior cavalry divisional commander when Sheridan was promoted to the Army of the Shenandoah. He inherited command of the Cavalry Corps.

Sheridan was never completely satisfied with Torbert's performance during the Valley Campaign, believing Torbert moved too slowly and that he lacked the aggressiveness needed in a cavalry commander. As a result, Sheridan gradually sidelined Torbert as the campaign progressed, increasingly relying on the cavalry's divisional commanders when independent action was needed.

Wesley Merritt experienced a meteoric rise during the Civil War. He ended the war as a brevet major-general commanding the Cavalry Corps. During the Shenandoah campaign Merritt commanded the Cavalry Corps' 1st Division. (AC)

Brigadier-General Wesley Merritt

Merritt commanded the 1st Division of the Cavalry Corps during Sheridan's Shenandoah campaign. Born in New York City, he attended West Point, graduating 22nd in a class of 41 in 1860. Despite the latter, upon graduation he received a commission in the cavalry. He served in cavalry units throughout the Civil War, participating in Stoneman's Raid that preceded Chancellorsville in 1863, and commanding the 2nd Cavalry at Brandy Station. Following the latter, he was promoted from captain to brigadier-general, and commanded a brigade in Buford's Division at Gettysburg. Following John Buford's death, Merritt assumed command of the division. Sheridan relied on Merritt, giving him increasing responsibility.

Brigadier-General James H. Wilson

Wilson commanded the 3rd Division of the Cavalry Corps during Sheridan's Shenandoah campaign. A native of Shawneetown, Illinois, Wilson also graduated from West Point in 1860, sixth in his class of 41. Although starting his career as an engineer, Wilson transferred to the cavalry in February 1864. He was a protégé of Ulysses Grant, having served with Grant from late 1862 onward. As with Sheridan, Wilson moved east and to higher command with Grant. Sheridan and Wilson mutually disliked each other, and the two experienced a stormy relationship during the Shenandoah campaign. Nonetheless, Wilson played an important role in its opening stages.

CONFEDERATE COMMANDERS

Lieutenant-General Jubal Anderson Early

In June 1864 Robert E. Lee detached Jubal Early and his corps from the Army of Northern Virginia and sent them to the Shenandoah. Taking charge of the troops already present, Early became commander of the Confederate Army of the Valley, a position he held until March 1865.

Early, a native of Virginia, attended the United States Military Academy at West Point, graduating 18th out of 50 in the class of 1837. Following graduation he received a commission in the artillery, and fought in the opening phase of the Second Seminole War (1835–42) as a second lieutenant in the 3rd US Artillery. Early left the army in 1838, successfully practicing law in Virginia and Mississippi until the Civil War started. He accepted a major's commission in the 1st Virginia Volunteers during the Mexican–American War (between 1847 and 1848), briefly interrupting his civilian career.

Robert E. Lee called Jubal A. Early "My old, bad man." Until he met Sheridan, no Union general had defeated him. (LOC)

While Early strongly opposed Virginia's secession at the convention in April 1861, he accepted a commission in the Confederate States Army after Virginia joined the Confederacy. He commanded the 24th Virginia Infantry at First Bull Run (First Manassas) in July, gaining promotion to brigadier-general.

Wounded at the Battle of Williamsburg in May 1862, he returned to the Army of Northern Virginia in time for the Seven Days Battle in late June. He commanded a brigade in Ewell's Division at the battles of Malvern Hill, Cedar Mountain, Second Bull Run (Second Manassas), and Antietam (Sharpsburg). During Antietam he gained command of Ewell's Division, when Alexander Lawton (who had taken over from the injured Ewell) was badly wounded. Lee retained Early, impressed by his performance.

Early also performed well at both Fredericksburg and Chancellorsville, stopping Meade's breakthrough at the former, and holding a corps led by General John Sedgwick with just 5,000 men at Marye's Heights. A similarly solid performance during the Gettysburg campaign, especially his independent commands during the opening stages, led Lee to promote Early to lieutenant-general and a corps command in May 1864. When Lee needed to reinforce the Shenandoah Valley following the Union's spring offensive, he sent Early, considering him capable of dealing with a complex situation independently. Lee's confidence was soon rewarded. Over the next two months, Early, despite being badly outnumbered by the Union army, swept the Northern forces out of the Shenandoah Valley, led a raid that reached the gates of Washington DC and successfully raided Pennsylvania. These were the last successful Confederate offensives in the East.

Short-tempered and bitter by temperament, he became increasingly so as he grew older. While at West Point, Early brawled with fellow cadet Lewis Armistead, a fight that led to Armistead's departure from the academy. His short temper led Lee to call Early "My old, bad man," yet Early's aggressiveness, his willingness to take the fight to the enemy and his ability to command troops independently led Lee to overlook his short fuze. Early also helped create the "Lost Cause" movement after the Civil War.

He was a fault-finder, which combined with an acid tongue and short temper made many of his subordinate generals dislike him. Common soldiers under his command, admiring his tenaciousness and (more importantly) his ability to fight and win when faced with long odds, viewed him with affection, calling him "Old Jube" or "Old Jubilee."

Lieutenant-General Richard H. Anderson
Anderson commanded a corps consisting of Kershaw's infantry and Fizhugh Lee's cavalry divisions sent by Lee to reinforce Early in August 1864. Born in South Carolina, Anderson attended West Point, graduating 40th in a class of 56 in 1842. Despite the low ranking, he entered the cavalry. He fought at Vera Cruz in the Mexican–American War, and was breveted for bravery. He resigned his commission in the United States Army when South Carolina seceded, accepting command of the 1st South Carolina Infantry. Although he missed the First Battle of Bull Run, he participated in virtually every other battle fought by the Army of Northern Virginia, rising to division commander by 1862. He took over Longstreet's corps after the latter's injury at the Battle of the Wilderness in 1864. He played only a peripheral role in the Valley Campaigns of 1864, as his corps was recalled in early September.

John B. Gordon had no military training or experience prior to the Civil War. Like Joshua Chamberlain in the Union army (to whom Gordon surrendered his command at Appomattox), Gordon demonstrated a natural aptitude as a military leader. He developed the Confederate plan of attack at Cedar Creek, and superseded Early as commander of II Corps by the war's end. (AC)

Major-General John B. Gordon
John B. Gordon commanded a division in Early's Corps during the 1864 Shenandoah campaign. Born in Upson County, Georgia, Gordon lacked any military education or experience prior to the Civil War. Elected captain by his company in a

Georgia regiment when the war began, he quickly rose in rank due to his natural talent and aggressive nature. Although not a Virginian, he won Lee's trust, and was given command of a division in May 1864. Gordon was the architect of the Confederate attack at Cedar Creek, although Early ignored Gordon's recommendation to press the attack once the Union camp had been taken.

Major-General Robert E. Rodes

A native of Virginia and an 1848 graduate of the Virginia Military Institute in Lexington, Rodes commanded a division in Early's Corps. An assistant professor at the institute from 1848 until 1851, he left after being passed over for promotion to full professor in favor of Thomas E. "Stonewall" Jackson. Trained as a civil engineer, he became chief engineer for the Alabama and Chattanooga Railroad in Tuscaloosa, Alabama. Adopting Alabama as home, upon the start of the Civil War he accepted command of an Alabama infantry regiment. He fought at most of the major battles in the Eastern Theater.

Although he lacked a West Point education, he rose quickly in the Army of Northern Virginia, gaining command of a division prior to Chancellorsville, and briefly commanded the attack on the Union XI Corps after Jackson was wounded. His division was moved to Ewell's corps when Lee reorganized the army after Chancellorsville. He commanded the division until his death at the Third Battle of Winchester on September 19, 1864.

Major-General Stephen D. Ramseur

Born in North Carolina, Stephen Ramseur commanded a division in Early's Corps during the Shenandoah campaigns of 1864. Along with his Union counterparts Wesley Merritt and James Wilson, Ramseur was a member of West Point's class of 1860, graduating 14th out of 41. An ardent secessionist, he joined the Confederate army prior to North Carolina joining the Confederacy. Given command of a North Carolina infantry regiment in 1861, he rose from colonel to major-general in three years. Highly talented, aggressive, and with an aptitude for placing his command in the critical point on the battlefield, he died at the Battle of Cedar Creek on October 19.

Major-General Joseph B. Kershaw

Kershaw commanded an infantry division sent by Lee to reinforce Early's Army of the Valley. Born in South Carolina, Kershaw was a lawyer and politician by

Robert Rodes commanded what had been Early's Division before the latter had been promoted to corps command. Rodes was killed at Third Winchester. His colleagues and superiors viewed him as a promising officer who died before achieving military greatness. (AC)

trade and training rather than a soldier. His only pre-war military experience was during the Mexican–American War, as a lieutenant in the Palmetto Regiment, a South Carolina volunteer unit. Following South Carolina's secession in 1861, he was made colonel of the 2nd South Carolina Infantry. He fought in most of the major battles in the Eastern Theater, from First Bull Run in 1861 through the Overland Campaign in 1864, and was also sent to Tennessee to participate in the Chickamauga campaign. His competence over the course of this period led to promotion. Given division command after Chickamauga, he was promoted to major-general in May 1864. Kershaw was one of only three divisional commanders in the Army of Northern Virginia without formal military training.

Major-General Lunsford L. Lomax

Lomax commanded Early's cavalry during much of Sheridan's Valley Campaign. Although born in Rhode Island, he was the son of a Virginian-born officer in the United States Army, and his allegiance was to his father's state. Lomax graduated from West Point in 1856, finishing 21st out of a class of 49, and served in the 2nd Cavalry following graduation. When the Civil War began, he resigned his army commission, and accepted an appointment in the Virginia state militia. His initial service was in the Western Theater, serving in staff positions for Joseph E. Johnston and Benjamin McCulloch. Transferred east, he was given command of the 11th Virginia Cavalry after Chancellorsville. He quickly rose in Lee's army. In August 1864 he was promoted to major-general, and served in the Shenandoah Valley commanding the cavalry there, including the irregular units.

Lunsford L. Lomax commanded the Confederate cavalry in the Valley District at the outset of Sheridan's campaign. He supervised the intelligence gathering and operations of Mosby's Rangers. (AC)

OPPOSING FORCES

As with the commanders, the troops in Sheridan's Shenandoah campaign were among the best soldiers available to both sides in 1864. At the beginning of the year, the troops in the Shenandoah had been leftovers—locally recruited, or simply shifted into the area and considered too unimportant to move to a more active theater. Grant's 1864 spring offensive, with simultaneous drives on several fronts—including into the Shenandoah Valley—underscored the importance of the valley to the South.

Lee countered the Northern threat by shifting Early's Corps to the valley. Among the best soldiers in Lee's army, Early and his men did what Lee expected them to do. Despite being outnumbered two to one by Union forces, the Confederates under Early swept the Union troops from the valley. Early even delivered a secondary objective of the transfer; his lightning raids into Pennsylvania and Washington DC drew troops away from Grant at Petersburg.

In a sense, Early was too successful. Given the skill of the Confederates guarding the valley, Grant realized that quantity alone would not yield victory. The valley was too important to cede to the South, however. The reinforcements Grant sent were among his best—men who had been tested in battle, and who performed reliably. Even troops drawn from other theaters, such as the XIX Corps' divisions brought from the Mississippi, were the best available. This, in turn, forced Lee to dispatch still more combat veterans to the valley. The loser in the upcoming contest might blame many factors for defeat—inadequate supplies, poor lines of communication, or even bad luck—but a lack of quality troops would be no valid excuse for failure. Neither side had to apologize for the troops in the campaign.

Washing day for an army on the march. Clean clothes and marching were equally important for soldiers in the Civil War, regardless of side. Men of both armies would remember days like this. (LOC)

UNION ARMY OF THE SHENANDOAH

Grant built the Union Army of the Shenandoah from four sources: the Army of West Virginia, the Army of the Potomac's VI Corps and the Cavalry Corps, and the Union's XIX Corps.

The Army of West Virginia was made up of the troops originally in the region, roughly two infantry divisions, one cavalry division, and an artillery brigade. These troops were commanded by major-generals Franz Sigel and David Hunter earlier in 1864. In August that year, these soldiers were reorganized into the Department of West Virginia. It contained 26,000 men: 14,000 infantry, 8,500 cavalry, and 3,500 artillerymen. A sizable percentage was required to guard West Virginia, western Maryland, western Virginia and the approaches to Pennsylvania. They were also needed to protect supply lines and communications and to guard against raiding Confederate partisan units. Thus, Sheridan could only use 60 percent of these men in his field army.

Sheridan reorganized these troops. He took roughly half the cavalry, creating one cavalry division, which he assigned to his Cavalry Corps as the 2nd Division. Of the infantry, he took 12,000 men, divided into three infantry divisions: the 1st, 2nd (Kanawha), and Provisional divisions. The 1st and 2nd divisions, existing formations, were used as field formations. The Provisional Division, made up of replacements and garrison troops, was kept as a reserve and rarely exceeded a brigade in strength. This force was designated the Army of West Virginia.

These troops may have been chased out of the valley by Early's offensive in June, but this represented a failure of army leadership, not a weakness among these soldiers. One infantry division—the Kanawha—had a distinguished combat history, and numbered among its officers two men that later became Presidents of the United States: Rutherford B. Hayes and William McKinley.

With a field force that ranged between 12,000 and 14,000 men, the Army of West Virginia was the size of a Union corps, and was treated as such tactically during Sheridan's campaign. Histories often refer to it as VIII Corps, perhaps confusing it with the actual formation of that name, commanded by Lew Wallace, which defended Washington DC.

Most of the rest of the Union Army of the Shenandoah was drawn from the Army of the Potomac. Grant had been forced to detach VI Corps to Washington as a result of Early's July raid. Rather than use it in static defense of the capital, Grant made virtue out of necessity. He gave VI Corps to Sheridan, to help clear Early out of the Shenandoah. Grant also threw in two divisions of the Army of the Potomac's Cavalry Corps.

VI Corps was one of the Union army's best corps. Organized in 1862, it had participated in most of the Army of the Potomac's campaigns, from George B. McClellan's 1862 Peninsula Campaign through Grant's Overland Campaign in 1864. At Gettysburg it was numerically the largest corps in the Union army.

Future President William McKinley enlisted as a private in the 23rd Ohio Infantry in 1861. By 1864 he had risen to the rank of captain. He served on Brigadier-General George Crook's staff during Sheridan's Shenandoah campaign. (AC)

After the Army of the Potomac's reorganization in spring 1864, VI Corps numbered over 24,000 men. VI Corps fought a hard campaign, and by August its numbers had been significantly reduced. Returns for August reported 16,414 officers and men present. The men who remained were experienced, long-term combat veterans. They knew how to fight, were steady in battle, and had survived some of the toughest engagements of the Civil War.

The rest of the Army of the Potomac's contribution came from the Cavalry Corps. For the first two years of the war the Cavalry Corps had performed poorly. Its results and reputation began to change in 1863, starting with the Battle of Brandy Station. It turned in a creditable performance at Gettysburg, seizing ground that allowed the Union army to gain a strong position running from the Round Tops to Culp's Hill. By August 1864, led by Phil Sheridan, the Cavalry Corps had been transformed into an elite formation.

The Union cavalry was of limited use in eastern Virginia while the Army of the Potomac was mired in a siege at Petersburg. It was ideal for the mobile warfare that an attack on the Shenandoah Valley involved, so Grant added two of its three divisions to Sheridan's forces, keeping one for himself. The 1st and 3rd divisions of the Cavalry Corps brought Sheridan over 11,000 officers and men, a combination of cavalry and attached horse artillery. With the cavalry from the Department of West Virginia added to this Cavalry Corps as its 2nd Division, Sheridan had one of the most formidable collections of horse soldiers available to the Union army for his campaign.

A private from the 67th Pennsylvania Regiment. The 67th Pennsylvania was assigned to the 2nd Brigade of the 3rd Division of VI Corps. (AC)

Finally, to bulk out the Army of the Shenandoah, Grant gave Sheridan two divisions from the United States Army's XIX Corps. The latter had been part of Nathaniel Banks's Army of the Mississippi. They fought at Port Hudson in 1863, and participated in the Red River Campaign in the spring of 1864.

The Red River Campaign ended disastrously, and XIX Corps had relatively little to do by summer. Grant decided its soldiers would be better used actively serving in the Virginia Theater than in reserve in a military backwater like Louisiana. Grant transferred two of its divisions east and they were on hand when he began organizing the new push in the Shenandoah. He gave the two divisions to Sheridan, providing the Army of the Shenandoah with an additional 14,000 infantry. These men were veteran troops, tested in battle.

These soldiers gave Sheridan a force of 45,000 men for his offensive, as well as reserves to draw upon in case of need. His troops were well supplied, well equipped and well armed. Most were men who had long-term enlistments. The majority, due to the units involved, were volunteers. Most were also combat veterans. Almost all had fought in the various Union spring 1864 offensives. Some were veterans of Chancellorsville and Gettysburg.

Most infantry units had late-model 1861 Springfield or 1853 Enfield rifled muskets. The Union cavalry were equipped with repeating rifles—a force multiplier. The rate of fire that repeating Henry or Spencer rifles wielded by Union cavalry troopers permitted a dismounted cavalry regiment to stop an advancing Confederate infantry brigade, despite the longer range of the infantry's rifles. Additionally, the Army of the Shenandoah had 100 artillery pieces assigned to its field corps. These were light cannon, capable of rapid movement.

The Union army was suffering from manpower problems by summer 1864. To make up a shortage of infantry, it had started to pull heavy artillery regiments out of their fortifications, strip these regiments of their artillery, and re-equip them as infantry. It was also dismounting surplus cavalry regiments and using these as ad hoc infantry. Grant had done his best to give Sheridan the best troops available, however. Of the nearly 100 regiments assigned to infantry brigades in the Army of the Shenandoah, only four were heavy artillery or dismounted cavalry.

One unusual aspect of the Union Army of the Shenandoah was an absence of "Colored" units. The Army of West Virginia was one of the few "all-white" armies in the Union order of battle by 1864. The Army of the Potomac had enough Colored regiments that it eventually formed a corps exclusively from Colored troops. XIX Corps was one of the first Union formations to field large numbers of these troops. Yet VI Corps was all white, as the two cavalry divisions detached from the Army of the Potomac (1st and 3rd) had no Colored cavalry regiments and the two divisions sent east from XIX Corps consisted solely of white soldiers.

An artillery private in the United States Army offers a stern-faced pose in a formal portrait. With his artillery sword at present and a pistol stuck in his belt, he attempts to impress the folks back home. (LOC)

Troopers of the 1st United States Cavalry Regiment at Brandy Station in February 1864. Six months later it formed part of Brigadier-General Wesley Merritt's 1st Cavalry Division, fighting in the Shenandoah Valley. (AC)

CONFEDERATE ARMY OF THE VALLEY

Opposing the Union forces was the Confederate Army of the Valley. At the start of the campaign this consisted of Jubal Early's corps augmented by the remaining Confederate field forces in the Shenandoah Valley at the end of the Union spring offensives. To offset the reinforcements sent to Sheridan, it was reinforced in August by a second corps sent from the Army of Northern Virginia. Lee intended this corps as a loan, however, to be returned at the earliest opportunity. In addition, Early could call upon the services of several regiments of partisan cavalry. These were locally raised formations, enrolled in the Confederate armies but fighting exclusively as guerrillas, attacking lines of communication.

Early and his corps had been shifted to the valley in June 1864, as Lee's response to the Union's spring offensives. Officially II Corps of the Army of Northern Virginia, by June 1864 it was almost universally called "Early's Corps." Organized in 1862, it was originally commanded by the legendary Thomas "Stonewall" Jackson. Following the latter's death at Chancellorsville in 1863, its command was inherited by Richard Ewell. Early took command on May 29, 1864, after Lee, dissatisfied with Ewell's performance as a corps commander, shuffled Ewell off to a backwater assignment.

Luther Hart Clapp of Company C, 37th Virginia Infantry Regiment. The 37th Virginia was part of Terry's Brigade in Gordon's Division. Terry's Brigade contained the remnants of 14 Virginia regiments decimated during the Overland Campaign. (LOC)

This corps had one of the most celebrated histories in the Army of Northern Virginia. It formed the core of "Jackson's Foot Cavalry" that hustled the Union out of the Shenandoah Valley in 1862. It led the flanking movement that routed the Union army at Chancellorsville. It smashed the Union garrison holding Winchester, Virginia at the Second Battle of Winchester in mid-June 1863.

By August 1864 the corps had been whittled down to three understrength infantry divisions. While its divisions officially listed 34,515 men on its rosters, those actually present totaled just over 10,000 men. On a good day those present for duty—excluding the sick and otherwise unavailable for fighting—might number between 8,200 and 8,300 men. The corps had three battalions of artillery, with 35 light field guns.

However, the soldiers present for combat were the best available. It included survivors from the old "Stonewall Brigade" (commanded by Jackson at First Bull Run). In 1864 it was leavened by the veterans of Jackson's campaigns and Gettysburg, and virtually all the men present in August had fought in the Overland Campaign, and in Early's offensives in the Shenandoah and the raids into Maryland, Pennsylvania and Washington DC that summer. The 10,000 that remained were among the most experienced troops left in the Army of Northern Virginia.

These troops were underfed, short on ammunition, and frequently had to fight barefoot in tattered uniforms or civilian clothing due to Confederate supply shortages. Yet fight they did. Since being detached from Lee's direct command, they chased the Yankees out of the Shenandoah Valley, twice raided Pennsylvania, burning Harrisburg, and drove the Union army into the fortifications guarding Washington DC.

Supplementing Early's Corps were troops originally stationed in the valley at the beginning of 1864. By August the field portion of this force had been reduced to the equivalent of a division each of infantry and cavalry and 13 pieces of field artillery. As with the men in Early's Corps, these soldiers were long-term veterans. The regiments assigned to the valley in 1864 were generally from western Virginia, including the Shenandoah counties and present-day West Virginia.

These men spent most of the war fighting in western Virginia, eastern Kentucky, and eastern Tennessee. These were the forces that had faced Franz Sigel's corps and David Hunter's Army of Western Virginia in the spring. They fought at New Market and Lynchburg earlier in the year, and were intimately familiar with the Shenandoah Valley. Their numbers were small—perhaps 2,500 to 3,000 infantry and 2,000 cavalry—but, as with Early's Corps, the ones that remained were the fighters.

These units were joined by two additional divisions under the command of Lieutenant-General Richard H. Anderson: Major-General Fitzhugh Lee's cavalry division and Major-General Joseph B. Kershaw's infantry division. Both had 20 field guns. Sent from the Army of Northern Virginia, Lee intended these troops as temporary reinforcements, to counter Sheridan's buildup. The cavalry division—with fewer than 2,000 men—remained in the valley for the rest of the campaign. Kershaw's Division, which numbered 3,800 at the end of August, was recalled to the Army of Northern Virginia in early September, only to be ordered back to the valley following the Third Battle of Winchester on September 19.

As with Early's Corps, the men from these two divisions were long-term veterans. Kershaw's Division had fought with the Army of Northern Virginia from the Peninsula Campaign in 1862 through the Overland Campaign in 1864. It was also part of Longstreet's Corps dispatched to Tennessee in the last half of 1863, and had fought at Chickamauga and participated in besieging Knoxville. The three brigades that made up the cavalry division rode with J.E.B. Stuart until his death in 1864. One regiment had had Stuart as their first colonel. Other regiments had participated in Jackson's Valley Campaign in 1862.

Bernard Bluecher Graves served in the Amherst Artillery, part of Nelson's Battalion. A corporal, Graves fought in most of the major battles during the Shenandoah campaign. He was captured at Waynesboro on March 2, 1865. (LOC)

A cavalry trooper from Brigadier-General Thomas Lafayette Rosser's Laurel Brigade. The Laurel Brigade was sent to the Shenandoah after Fisher's Hill to reinforce the Confederate cavalry in Early's army. (LOC)

The Army of the Valley was "white." Most of its soldiers came from farming backgrounds, many from small family farms. Their absence meant hardship for their families. Relatively few owned slaves.

In total, Early could field no more than 20,000 men during Sheridan's Valley Campaign. Frequently, he could only muster 10,000 or fewer men. Nor could he expect replacements for his losses. The Confederacy's manpower barrel was empty. Yet Early's troops still gave him a few advantages. Many were familiar with the terrain they were fighting over. All were tough—three years of hard fighting had scoured away the weak, lame, and lazy. Those still fighting were fiercely loyal to their states. Those that were not had gone home.

Two final units that bear mention are two partisan cavalry battalions: Lieutenant-Colonel John S. Mosby's Rangers or Raiders (43rd Battalion Virginia Cavalry) and Captain John H. McNeill's Rangers (Company E of the 18th Virginia Cavalry). They were not present at the major battles during Sheridan's Valley Campaign, and between them never fielded more than 650 men. Yet both had an influence disproportionate to their tables of organization.

The Southern States raised several dozen partisan cavalry regiments and battalions in the early years of the Civil War. These units were intended to

Colonel John S. Mosby and 16 members of the 43rd Virginia Cavalry Battalion—better known as Mosby's Rangers. Mosby is the fourth figure from the left in the second row, sitting with his legs crossed. (AC)

operate behind Union lines as irregulars, disrupting Union supply lines and communications. Lee's unease with guerrilla warfare caused most partisan units to be disbanded or reorganized as standard cavalry at the start of 1864. Only Mosby's Rangers and McNeill's Rangers, both in Virginia's western counties, were retained as partisans.

These battalions operated in small groups of 30 to 150 men, generally at night, and attacked Union lines of communications. They fought in uniform, but the uniforms were informal. In some cases, gray clothing sufficed. They blended into the civilian population when not fighting, and permitted civilians, not formally enlisted, to accompany them on raids. A relative handful, they tied down tens of thousands of Union troops in protecting railroads, depots, and telegraph lines. The Union army considered them guerrillas and illegal combatants, not entitled to protection as prisoners of war when captured.

These rangers made a significant contribution to Early's ability to hold the Shenandoah Valley by denying Sheridan's field army the troops required to protect Union lines. Yet they also contributed significantly to the bitterness with which Sheridan's Valley Campaign was fought. The presence of partisan rangers in the Union rear was a major reason for Sheridan's decision to burn the valley out in September and October 1864.

ORDER OF BATTLE

UNION ARMY OF THE SHENANDOAH
6th United States Cavalry (Escort)

VI ARMY CORPS
1st Michigan Cavalry, Co. G (Escort)
1st Division
1st Brigade
  4th New Jersey
  10th New Jersey
  15th New Jersey
2nd Brigade
  2nd Connecticut Heavy Artillery
  65th New York
  121st New York
  95th Pennsylvania[1]
  96th Pennsylvania[1]
3rd Brigade[2]
  37th Massachusetts
  49th Pennsylvania
  82nd Pennsylvania
  119th Pennsylvania
  2nd Rhode Island (battalion)
  5th Wisconsin (battalion)
2nd Division
1st Brigade

62nd New York
93rd Pennsylvania
98th Pennsylvania
102nd Pennsylvania
139th Pennsylvania
2nd Brigade
  2nd Vermont
  3rd Vermont
  4th Vermont
  5th Vermont
  6th Vermont
  11th Vermont
3rd Brigade
  7th Maine[3]
  49th New York
  77th New York
  122nd New York
  61st Pennsylvania (battalion)

3rd Division
1st Brigade
  14th New Jersey
  106th New York
  151st New York
  184th New York (battalion)[4]
  87th Pennsylvania[4]
  10th Vermont

2nd Brigade
  6th Maryland
  9th New York Heavy Artillery
  110th Ohio
  122nd Ohio
  126th Ohio
  67th Pennsylvania
  138th Ohio
Artillery Brigade
  Maine Light Artillery, 5th Battery (E)
  Massachusetts Light Artillery, 1st Battery (A)
  1st Rhode Island Light Artillery, Battery C
  1st Rhode Island Light Artillery, Battery G
  1st United States Artillery, Battery M

XIX ARMY CORPS
1st Division
1st Brigade
  29th Maine
  30th Massachusetts
  90th New York[5]
  114th New York
  116th New York

153rd New York

2nd Brigade

    12th Connecticut

    160th New York

    121st New York[6]

    47th Pennsylvania

    4th Vermont

3rd Brigade[7]

    30th Maine

    133rd New York

    162nd New York

    165th New York

    173rd New York

Artillery

    New York Light Artillery, 5th Battery

2nd Division

1st Brigade

    9th Connecticut

    12th Maine

    14th Maine

    26th Massachusetts

    14th New Hampshire

    75th New York

2nd Brigade

    13th Connecticut

    11th Indiana

    22nd Iowa

    3rd Massachusetts Cavalry (dismounted)

    131st New York

    159th New York

3rd Brigade

    38th Massachusetts

    128th New York

    156th New York

    175th New York

    176th New York

4th Brigade

    8th Indiana

    18th Indiana

    24th Iowa

    28th Iowa

Artillery

    Maine Light Artillery, 1st Battery (A)

Reserve artillery

    Indiana Light Artillery, 17th Battery

    1st Rhode Island Light Artillery, Battery D

ARMY OF WEST VIRGINIA (VIII ARMY CORPS)

1st Division

1st Brigade

    34th Massachusetts

    5th New York Heavy Artillery, 2nd Battalion

    116th Ohio

    123rd Ohio

2nd Brigade[1,2]

    1st West Virginia

    4th West Virginia

    12th West Virginia

3rd Brigade

    23rd Illinois (battalion)

    54th Pennsylvania

    10th West Virginia

    11th West Virginia

    15th West Virginia

2nd Division

1st Brigade

    23rd Ohio

    36th Ohio

    5th West Virginia

    13th West Virginia

2nd Brigade

    34th Ohio (battalion)

    91st Ohio

    9th West Virginia

    14th West Virginia

Brigadier-General George R. Crook replaced David Hunter as the commander of the Army of West Virginia in August 1864. The army's cavalry was reassigned to the Army of the Shenandoah's Cavalry Corps, leaving Crook in operational charge of two full-strength and one brigade-sized infantry divisions. (LOC)

Artillery Brigade

- 1st Ohio Light Artillery, Battery L
- 1st Pennsylvania Light Artillery, Battery D
- 1st Rhode Island Light Artillery, Battery G[6]
- 5th United States Artillery, Battery B

CAVALRY CORPS

1st Rhode Island Cavalry (Escort)

1st Division

1st Brigade
- 1st Michigan Cavalry
- 5th Michigan Cavalry
- 6th Michigan Cavalry
- 7th Michigan Cavalry
- 25th Michigan Cavalry[6]

2nd Brigade
- 4th New York Cavalry
- 6th New York Cavalry
- 9th New York Cavalry
- 19th New York Cavalry (1st Dragoons)
- 17th Pennsylvania Cavalry[8]

3rd Brigade[9]
- 1st Maryland Potomac Home Brigade
- 2nd Massachusetts Cavalry
- 25th New York Cavalry

Reserve Brigade
- 19th New York (1st Dragoons) Cavalry
- 6th Pennsylvania Cavalry[6]

- 1st United States Cavalry
- 2nd United States Cavalry
- 5th United States Cavalry

2nd Division

1st Brigade
- 8th Ohio Cavalry (detachment)
- 14th Pennsylvania Cavalry
- 22nd Pennsylvania Cavalry

2nd Brigade
- 1st New York Cavalry
- 1st West Virginia Cavalry
- 2nd West Virginia Cavalry
- 3rd West Virginia Cavalry

Artillery
- 5th United States Artillery, Battery L

3rd Division

1st Brigade
- 1st Connecticut Cavalry
- 3rd New Jersey Cavalry
- 2nd New York Cavalry
- 5th New York Cavalry
- 2nd Ohio Cavalry
- 18th Pennsylvania Cavalry

2nd Brigade
- 3rd Indiana Cavalry
- 1st New Hampshire Cavalry
- 8th New York Cavalry
- 22nd New York Cavalry
- 1st Vermont Cavalry

Horse Artillery
- New York Light Artillery, 6th Battery[10]
- 1st United States Artillery, Battery K

and Battery L[11]
- 2nd United States Artillery, Battery B and Battery L
- 2nd United States Artillery, Battery D
- 2nd United States Artillery, Battery M
- 3rd United States Artillery, Battery C, Battery F, and Battery K
- 4th United States Artillery, Battery C and Battery E

Notes on Union forces

1. Guarding trains during the the Third Battle of Winchester (September 19) and not engaged in the battle.
2. At Winchester during the Battle of Cedar Creek (October 19).
3. Replaced by 1st Maine (Veteran) Infantry after the Third Battle of Winchester.
4. One battalion of the 184th New York replaced one battalion of the 87th Pennsylvania after the Third Battle of Winchester.
5. Added after September 20.
6. Detached after September 20.
7. In reserve at Harpers Ferry during the Third Battle of Winchester (September 19).
8. Assigned to 3rd Brigade, 1st Division, VI Corps during the Battle of Cedar Creek (October 19).
9. Dissolved September 9.
10. Assigned to 1st Brigade, 1st Division, Cavalry Corps after September 20.
11. Assigned to 2nd Brigade, 1st Division, Cavalry Corps after September 20.

Company D of the 6th Pennsylvania Cavalry was part of the 1st Cavalry Division during Sheridan's campaign in the Shenandoah. (AC)

CONFEDERATE ARMY OF THE VALLEY

II CORPS (EARLY'S CORPS), ARMY OF NORTHERN VIRGINIA

Rodes's (later Ramseur's) Division

Grimes's Brigade
- 32nd North Carolina Infantry
- 43rd North Carolina Infantry
- 45th North Carolina Infantry
- 53rd North Carolina Infantry
- 2nd North Carolina Infantry Battalion (independent)

Cox's Brigade
- 1st North Carolina Infantry
- 2nd North Carolina Infantry
- 3rd North Carolina Infantry
- 4th North Carolina Infantry
- 14th North Carolina Infantry
- 30th North Carolina Infantry

Cook's Brigade
- 4th Georgia Infantry
- 12th Georgia Infantry
- 21st Georgia Infantry
- 44th Georgia Infantry

Battle's Brigade
- 3rd Alabama Infantry
- 5th Alabama Infantry
- 6th Alabama Infantry
- 12th Alabama Infantry
- 61st Alabama Infantry

Gordon's Division

Hays's Brigade
- 5th Louisiana Infantry
- 6th Louisiana Infantry
- 7th Louisiana Infantry
- 8th Louisiana Infantry
- 9th Louisiana Infantry

Evans's Brigade
- 13th Georgia Infantry
- 26th Georgia Infantry
- 31st Georgia Infantry
- 60th Georgia Infantry
- 61st Georgia Infantry
- 12th Georgia Infantry Battalion (independent)

Stafford's Brigade
- 1st Louisiana Infantry
- 2nd Louisiana Infantry
- 10th Louisiana Infantry
- 14th Louisiana Infantry
- 15th Louisiana Infantry

Terry's Brigade
- 2nd Virginia Infantry
- 4th Virginia Infantry
- 5th Virginia Infantry
- 27th Virginia Infantry
- 33rd Virginia Infantry
- 21st Virginia Infantry
- 25th Virginia Infantry
- 42nd Virginia Infantry
- 44th Virginia Infantry
- 48th Virginia Infantry
- 50th Virginia Infantry
- 10th Virginia Infantry
- 23rd Virginia Infantry
- 37th Virginia Infantry

Ramseur's (later Pegram's) Division

Pegram's Brigade
- 13th Virginia Infantry
- 31st Virginia Infantry
- 49th Virginia Infantry
- 52rd Virginia Infantry
- 58th Virginia Infantry

Johnston's Brigade
- 5th North Carolina Infantry
- 12th North Carolina Infantry
- 20th North Carolina Infantry
- 23rd North Carolina Infantry

Godwin's Brigade
- 6th North Carolina Infantry
- 21st North Carolina Infantry
- 54th North Carolina Infantry
- 57th North Carolina Infantry
- 1st North Carolina Infantry Battalion (independent)

Artillery Division
- Braxton's Battalion
- Cutshaw's Battalion
- McLaughlin's (later King's) Battalion
- Nelson's Battalion

Breckinridge's (later Wharton's) Division

Wharton's Brigade
- 45th Virginia Infantry
- 50th Virginia Infantry
- 51st Virginia Infantry
- 30th Virginia Infantry Battalion, Sharpshooters

Echol's Brigade
- 22nd Virginia Infantry
- 23rd Virginia Infantry Battalion (independent)
- 26th Virginia Infantry Battalion (independent)

Smith's Brigade
- 36th Virginia Infantry
- 60th Virginia Infantry
- 45th Virginia Infantry Battalion (independent)
- Thomas Legion

Lomax's Division (Cavalry)

Imboden's Brigade
- 18th Virginia Cavalry
- 23rd Virginia Cavalry
- 62nd Virginia Cavalry

McCausland's Brigade
- 14th Virginia Cavalry
- 16th Virginia Cavalry
- 17th Virginia Cavalry
- 25th Virginia Cavalry
- 37th Virginia Cavalry Battalion (independent)

Bradley T. Johnson's Brigade
- 8th Virginia Cavalry
- 21st Virginia Cavalry
- 22nd Virginia Cavalry
- 34th Virginia Cavalry Battalion (independent)
- 36th Virginia Cavalry Battalion (independent)

Jackson's Brigade
- 2nd Maryland Cavalry
- 19th Virginia Cavalry
- 20th Virginia Cavalry
- 46th Virginia Cavalry Battalion (independent)
- 47th Virginia Cavalry Battalion (independent)

UNITS FROM I CORPS (ANDERSON'S CORPS)[1]

Kershaw's Division[2]

Conner's Brigade
- 2nd South Carolina Infantry
- 3rd South Carolina Infantry
- 7th South Carolina Infantry
- 8th South Carolina Infantry
- 15th South Carolina Infantry
- 20th South Carolina Infantry
- 3rd South Carolina Infantry Battalion (independent)

Wofford's Brigade

16th Georgia Infantry
18th Georgia Infantry
24th Georgia Infantry
3rd Georgia Infantry
Cobb's Legion (Georgia)
Phillips's Legion (Georgia)
Humphrey's Brigade
13th Mississippi Infantry
17th Mississippi Infantry
18th Mississippi Infantry
21st Mississippi Infantry
Bryan's Brigade
10th Georgia Infantry
50th Georgia Infantry
51st Georgia Infantry
53rd Georgia Infantry
Fitzhugh Lee's Division (Cavalry)
Wickham's Brigade
1st Virginia Cavalry
2nd Virginia Cavalry
3rd Virginia Cavalry

4th Virginia Cavalry
Rosser's (Laurel) Brigade[3]
7th Virginia Cavalry
11th Virginia Cavalry
12th Virginia Cavalry
35th Virginia Cavalry Battalion
(independent)
Payne's Brigade
5th Virginia Cavalry
6th Virginia Cavalry
15th Virginia Cavalry
Artillery
Carter's Battalion
Horse Artillery (seven batteries)
Independent partisan ranger units in theater
43rd Virginia Cavalry Battalion (Mosby's
Raiders)
McNeill's Virginia Cavalry Company
(McNeill's Rangers)

Notes on Confederate forces

1. Sent to the valley on August 15, 1864.
2. Withdrawn September 14, 1864; ordered back, September 20.
3. Initially remained with the Army of Northern Virginia after Lee's Division was sent to the valley. Ordered to the valley on September 20, 1864 from the Petersburg theater.

Major-General Joseph Kershaw commanded a division temporarily sent by Lee to reinforce the Army of the Valley. Kershaw's Division was on its way back to Petersburg at the Third Battle of Winchester. It missed that battle as well as Fisher's Hill, but rejoined Early in late September at Browns Gap (AC).

OPPOSING PLANS

On August 1, 1864 General Grant outlined the following objectives for Sheridan in the Shenandoah Valley: "I want Sheridan put in command of all the troops in the field, with instructions to put himself south of the enemy and follow him to the death. Wherever the enemy goes let our troops go also. Once started up the valley they ought to be followed until we get possession of the Virginia Central Railroad."

Grant viewed Sheridan's objectives as threefold:

1. Destroy Jubal Early's Army of the Valley;
2. Deny the Confederacy the resources of the Shenandoah Valley;
3. Cut the Virginia Central Railroad.

Early's army posed a threat to Washington and to Union supporters in Pennsylvania and Maryland. It was also the last major source of reinforcements for the Army of Northern Virginia. Destroying it would simultaneously remove the threat to Union territory, wrest control of the Shenandoah from the Confederacy, and deny Lee additional troops to defend Petersburg.

The Shenandoah fed the Army of Northern Virginia, providing horses to remount its cavalry and pull its supply wagons and artillery caissons. Controlling the valley would not only deny these resources to the Confederacy, but also potentially make them available to the Union.

As Early demonstrated, the Shenandoah provided a route for the South to invade Maryland and Pennsylvania. Union control of at least the lower Shenandoah Valley would block that route, even if Early's army remained. A Confederate army advancing northward without Confederate control of the lower Shenandoah Valley courted destruction.

With Petersburg besieged, the Virginia Central Railroad was one of only two railroads allowing access to Richmond that was unthreatened by Northern armies. Union possession of the Virginia Central at Charlottesville would force all rail traffic onto the already overloaded Richmond and Danville Railroad.

While Sheridan had clear and simply stated objectives, none were easily accomplished. Access to the Shenandoah Valley was limited. Union armies could move through the mouth of the valley, where the Shenandoah met the Potomac. The Blue Ridge Mountains were pierced at a dozen points with gaps allowing movement into the valley, most of which were small. Only the Manassas Gap, used by the Manassas Gap Railroad, the Rockfish Gap, through which the Virginia Central passed, and possibly the Swift Run Gap could be used by large formations or as reliable supply routes. The rest were more suited to the passage of a brigade than a corps.

The gaps were more useful as conduits than as invasion routes. Moreover, they were easy to defend; forcing a gap against a determined enemy would be a formidable task. Either side could be flanked by an attack through a gap, but except for the gaps north of Manassas Gap, the conduits favored movement of Confederate troops rather than Union forces. Since the Union forces were moving south, deep into Confederate territory, they had more to fear from the gaps than the Confederates.

Movement through the Valley and Ridge Appalachians on the west side of the Shenandoah was even more constrained. The passes were narrower, and the terrain to the west was rugged, lightly inhabited, and made traveling difficult. It offered few river, road, or rail routes by which a Northern army could be supplied.

The United States Armory and Arsenal at Harpers Ferry and the Baltimore & Ohio Railroad's yard and railroad bridge gave Harpers Ferry strategic importance. At the mouth of the Shenandoah Valley, it formed the starting point for any Union offensive in the Shenandoah. (AC)

Within the valley, supply would be an issue for both sides. The Winchester & Potomac Railroad ran from Harpers Ferry to Winchester. The Manassas Gap Railroad ran from Manassas Junction to Strasburg and Mount Jackson in the Middle Valley. The Virginia Central Railroad cut the upper valley through Staunton, Fishersville, and Waynesboro. The Union could use the Winchester & Potomac and the Manassas Gap railroads for supply, although both were inoperable by 1864. Even if placed in operation, both, but especially the Manassas Gap line, were subject to raiding. Although the Virginia Central, used by the Confederacy, was protected from Union assault, it was a long way from the lower valley, where fighting was expected.

The 50 miles (80km) between Mount Jackson and Staunton had to be supplied by wagon train. This would be more of a hardship to the Union than the Confederacy. The Union army, in hostile territory, had to provide its soldiers with everything from beans to bullets. In contrast, Confederate forces could draw upon food and fodder provided by sympathetic locals, and only needed to transport ammunition. Given that the Confederate stores of uniforms and military equipment were virtually non-existent, it left the commissariat with nothing to move.

Given those realities, Sheridan's approach was limited to the obvious route through the lower valley, following the course of the Shenandoah River, or going through the Manassas Gap. He could supplement either approach by sending additional forces through the northern Blue Ridge Mountain gaps to provide a flanking threat.

Union flanking forces would be limited to cavalry or perhaps a division of infantry at a gap. Sheridan had to be cautious about splitting his army, however. Using converging Union columns to attack Early was to invite defeat in detail. Early was in the central position and could strike out at a Union detachment with superior forces. Sheridan had no intention of repeating the mistakes of previous Union generals.

While Sheridan used broad strategic flanking movements before—most notably during his raid on Richmond that spring—ultimately he rejected a strategic flanking maneuver to open his Shenandoah offensive. He decided to strike south through the mouth of the valley. He would make tactical use of flanking movements though gaps and passes throughout the campaign, however.

Sheridan's plan to use this route was an obvious one, because of its strength. Moving through the Manassas Gap required Sheridan to either expose Harpers Ferry or to split his army. If he left Harpers Ferry open, he invited Early to reprise his summer raids against Pennsylvania and Washington. If he left enough troops at Harpers Ferry to discourage another raid, he would split the army into two bodies roughly equal to what Early was believed to have. (Union intelligence credited the Army of the Valley with double its actual forces.)

Sheridan might have been willing to fight Early on equal terms with an army that he had previously commanded and which he felt had confidence in him. Except for the two divisions he brought with him from the Army of the Potomac's Cavalry Corps, he had never led any of the men in his new command. He knew VI Corps, as Sheridan had fought alongside this unit during the Overland Campaign. The rest of the units in his army were new to him.

Sheridan had other constraints droving him to a direct approach. The first involved logistics. The longer his supply lines were, the easier they were to interdict. Sheridan appreciated the importance of secure supply lines; his division had been besieged in Chattanooga following the Battle of Chickamauga.

Union forces found it difficult merely to secure the Baltimore & Ohio running through Union-held Maryland and West Virginia. Protecting the Winchester & Potomac, which followed the direct line of advance up the valley, offered significant additional challenges. Using the Manassas Gap Railroad would be almost impossible; it lay dangerously close to the frontier between the two contesting sides and offered Confederate partisan raiders multiple new opportunities to attack Yankee weak points

Finally, in the opening phase of his offensive Sheridan was cautioned to not risk battle unless he was certain of victory. In part this instruction reflected the uncase that many senior officers and administration officials felt at having Sheridan leading an army in what was a vital offensive. He was extremely junior to hold such high command. His past record, while solid, also held hints he might not be up to the job, Grant's confidence notwithstanding.

It was more than just that, however. The Union simply could not afford another embarrassing debacle anywhere, but especially not in the Shenandoah Valley. The South was losing militarily, but it had not yet lost. Union military leaders believed (and Confederate officers feared) the North could batter the South into submission with another six months' hard fighting. Certainly a year would be sufficient.

Carl von Clausewitz states war is politics by other means, and the South could still win using politics as war by other means. The public had become war weary by 1864. The United States was holding national elections in November that year, in which Lincoln and his Republican Party were being opposed by a Democratic Party running on a peace platform. Should Lincoln lose the presidency, especially if the election yielded Democratic majorities in Congress, the South could win independence by negotiating with a new administration.

Railroads were critical to both sides for moving supplies and troops during the Civil War. The Baltimore & Ohio Railroad crossed in and around the Shenandoah Valley. Railroad access defined the battlefield. (AC)

Keeping an army in the field meant more than beating the enemy on the battlefield. It meant providing the logistics to support them in camp in the periods between battles. The ability to maintain an army was as important as its fighting ability. (AC)

The Union's spring offensives in 1864 had divided into three categories: disastrous (Red River and Shenandoah), frustratingly inconclusive (Atlanta), or horrifyingly bloody (the Overland Campaign). In August 1864 Lincoln's chances of re-election were evenly balanced. Another military disaster could tip victory to his opponents. Clearing the Confederates from the valley was important, but still more important was preventing another debacle which would further erode public confidence.

Thus, Sheridan had to fight the campaign using plans developed by others. It was best stated in orders Grant prepared for Major-General David Hunter prior to Sheridan's taking command and which Grant gave Sheridan when the latter accepted his new position. They read:

GENERAL: Concentrate all your available force without delay in the vicinity of Harpers Ferry, leaving only such railroad guards and garrisons for public property as may be necessary …

Use in this concentration the railroad, if by so doing time can be saved. From Harpers Ferry, if it is found that the enemy has moved north of the Potomac in large force, push north, following and attacking him wherever found; following him, if driven south of the Potomac, as long as it is safe to do so. If it is ascertained that the enemy has but a small force north of the Potomac, then push south the main force, detaching, under a competent commander, a sufficient force to look after the raiders and drive them to their homes.

In pushing up the Shenandoah Valley, as it is expected you will have to go first or last, it is desirable that nothing should be left to invite the enemy to return. Take all provisions, forage, and stock wanted for the use of your command. Such as cannot be consumed, destroy. It is not desirable that the buildings should be destroyed—they should, rather, be protected; but the people should be informed that so long as an army can subsist among them recurrences of these raids must be expected, and we are determined to stop them at all hazards.

Bear in mind, the object is to drive the enemy south; and to do this you want to keep him always in sight. Be guided in your course by the course he takes.

Make your own arrangements for supplies of all kinds, giving regular vouchers for such as may be taken from loyal citizens in the country through which you march.

Very respectfully,
U. S. GRANT, Lieut.-General.

Sheridan would be guided by these instructions, but did not feel bound to blindly obey them. He never advanced as far south in the valley as Grant desired. Sheridan pointedly ignored repeated suggestions to take the Virginia Central Railroad during the campaign. He finally took the railroad well after the campaign ended, and then only because it was on his army's route to the Army of the Potomac, which he wished to rejoin so as to be in at the death of the Army of Northern Virginia.

Sheridan's reluctance was due to his realization that the Army of the Shenandoah could not be supplied over the 50-mile gap between Mount Jackson and Staunton unless the Army of the Valley was destroyed. Otherwise there was too much risk of being isolated. Even then, Confederate guerrillas could still interdict supply lines.

Jubal Early's plans were virtually the mirror image of Phil Sheridan's. Early's goals remained unchanged: hold the Shenandoah Valley for the South, keep his army intact, threaten Maryland and Pennsylvania, and embarrass the North whenever possible. As long as Early was achieving his goals, Sheridan would be denied his.

From Early's perspective, the reconstituted Union Army of the Shenandoah changed nothing in his planning. Much of Sheridan's army was made up of the same soldiers Early had defeated in the recent past. Most of the reinforcements came from the Army of the Potomac, a known quantity for Early. He considered troops from that army to be slow moving, unaggressive, and unenthusiastic fighters. While good on the defense—the only battle in which they clearly licked the Army of Northern Virginia was Gettysburg, where the Army of the Potomac fought defensively—Sheridan's troops had to attack him. The rest of the Union forces had fought in the Red River Campaign, where they had been ignominiously routed.

Yet, the Union army vastly outnumbered Early's own men. Including troops used for guarding camps and communications, the Union could muster nearly six times as many soldiers as Early's command. Even counting just the forces Sheridan would take to the field, Early was outnumbered at least three to one.

Early had faced long odds before and emerged triumphant, most recently in his raid on Washington DC. While the Yankee had the numbers, Early believed he had superior mobility, a better knowledge of the terrain over which the battle was to be fought, and superior intelligence as to the location of enemy forces. If he could catch part of the enemy's force isolated, and

A major reason Sheridan chose to abandon the upper Shenandoah Valley once he had taken it was due to logistics. To maintain an army in Harrisonburg, 70 miles (110km) from his railhead in Winchester, required miles-long wagon trains, escorted by up to 2,000 soldiers. (AC)

attack that detachment with superior numbers, it did not matter how many total men the enemy had. Early felt that this new Union offensive would offer those types of opportunities, and was willing to bet he could capitalize on them.

If Early had one real fear, it was that the Union would attempt a wide flanking attack, attacking his rear. He wrote in his memoirs:

> If Sheridan had thrown his whole force on my lines of communications I would have been compelled to attempt to cut my way through as there was no escape for me to the right or left and my force was too weak to cross the Potomac while he was in my rear. If I had moved up the valley at all, I could not have stopped short of New Market, for between that place and the country in which I was there was no forage for my horses.

Sheridan was precluded from doing that due to orders issued to him, so Jubal Early's fears went unrealized. When Sheridan did simply move south from Harpers Ferry, and did so in a tentative manner, it confirmed Early's belief that Sheridan was just another typical Northern general. Like David Hunter and Franz Sigel, Sheridan would prove unimaginative, timid, and easily bluffed. Given that, Early felt that he could outmaneuver Sheridan, and trap Sheridan's army just as he had snared Hunter and Sigel. He also believed that if he gave Sheridan a bloody nose, Sheridan would withdraw, just as his predecessors had.

It was a dangerous miscalculation of Phil Sheridan's capabilities and temperament, one that ultimately proved fatal to the Army of the Valley. In a sense, the greatest weakness in Jubal Early's plans had their seed in Early's previous success that summer. For perhaps the first time in his career, Early was underestimating his opponent. With the odds stacked against his army as they were, Early had no margin for that type of error.

Martinsburg, West Virginia was the effective railhead for Union forces in the Shenandoah Valley, for most of the Valley Campaigns in 1864. The Baltimore & Ohio main line ran through Martinsburg. While the Winchester & Potomac reached Winchester, it could not be used until after Fisher's Hill, when the region between Winchester and Harpers Ferry was finally secured. (LOC)

THE CAMPAIGN

Although Sheridan's Valley Campaign technically ran from August through December 1864, it was all but over by mid-October. The brevity of the campaign was due to the swift achievement of two of its primary objectives: control of the Shenandoah Valley, and destruction of Confederate forces therein. Officially, Sheridan's Army of the Shenandoah and Early's Army of the Valley remained in the Shenandoah Valley until the end of February 1865, but both were a shadow of their former strengths by then. Each side began a drawdown of forces almost immediately after the decisive Union victory at Cedar Creek on October 19, 1864.

The campaign broke down into five phases. The opening phase ran from August 7, 1864, when Sheridan took command of the Middle Military Division until mid-September. This phase was characterized by cautious probing by both sides, as the two opposing commanders began to feel out the other commander's strengths and weaknesses.

The second phase was initiated by an opportunity seized by Sheridan when Early's army was weakened by the recall of Kershaw's Division to the Army of Northern Virginia. Running from September 16 to the 20th, it culminated in the Union victory at the Third Battle of Winchester.

The follow-up to the battle at Winchester formed the third phase of the campaign. Early established a new defensive position at Fisher's Hill. Sheridan's subordinates found a way to flank this position. Over three days (September 21–23) the two armies fought another major battle that yielded a further decisive Union victory.

The fourth phase covered the three-week period following the Battle of Fisher's Hill. Early was forced to withdraw to the upper valley. Although the period saw some cavalry skirmishing, most notably at the Battle of Toms Brook on October 9, there were no major clashes between

Sheridan's offensive opened with the cavalry riding out of the fortifications at Harpers Ferry. This image and others like it are pencil roughs by combat artist A.R. Waud. (LOC)

the main bodies of the armies. Instead, Sheridan began a systematic destruction of the strategic assets of the upper valley. Over the period known as "The Burning," Sheridan drew north, conducting a scorched-earth campaign where he set fire to garnered grain and fodder and destroyed public buildings. His goal was to eliminate the Shenandoah Valley's capability to supply the Confederacy.

The fifth and final phase was the period between October 16 and October 20, which culminated in the Battle of Cedar Creek. Jubal Early attempted one last ambush of the Union army. While his original attack was extraordinarily successful, what should have been a decisive Confederate victory was converted into an even more decisive Union triumph due to a late-afternoon counterattack, personally led by Phil Sheridan.

THE OPENING STAGES, AUGUST 7–SEPTEMBER 15

Philip Sheridan arrived at Monocacy, Virginia on August 6, 1864. The next day he took command of the Middle Military Division and the Army of the Shenandoah. On that date, the troops available for his use were the three divisions of VI Corps, one division and eight regiments from XIX Corps, one cavalry division and one cavalry brigade from the Army of the Potomac, and two infantry divisions from the Army of West Virginia. The remainder of his forces (two understrength West Virginia cavalry divisions, the rest of XIX Corps, and the remainder of the Army of the Potomac cavalry) would join Sheridan over the next three weeks. The army was not fully assembled until August 31.

Early was finishing up another of the raids he continued to launch from the Shenandoah, sending his cavalry into Pennsylvania. His men burned Chambersburg on July 30, destroying most of the town, including homes. As they withdrew, foraging parties gathered grain from the Sharpsburg area.

Sheridan opened the campaign by sending his cavalry ahead to screen his army. The 1st and 3rd Cavalry were sent probing down the passes of the Blue Ridge Mountains as far south as Manassas Gap. (LOC)

These actions mirrored similar actions by Sheridan's army as the campaign progressed, ones that were heavily criticized by the Confederates.

From Monocacy Sheridan moved his infantry to Halltown and sent cavalry to cut off Early's forces north of the Potomac. Even before this, learning of Sheridan's appointments and the new Union forces concentrated against him, Early began withdrawing his troops from Maryland and Pennsylvania. They were intercepted by Sheridan's 2nd Cavalry Division, commanded by Brigadier-General William Averell, on August 7. In the subsequent battle, despite being outnumbered nearly two to one, the Yankee cavalry captured nearly 400 Confederates, and wounded or killed nearly 100 more. In exchange, the Union only suffered 31 casualties. It would be the last time Early would move north of the Potomac.

Over the next week Sheridan positioned infantry in Charles Town, West Virginia and Berryville, Virginia, screening their positions from Early with his cavalry. Early concentrated his army at Bunker Hill, West Virginia, halfway between Hagerstown, Maryland and Winchester, Virginia. Realizing he was being flanked by Sheridan, Early abandoned Bunker Hill on August 10, falling back to Fisher's Hill. Sheridan now began probing with his cavalry. Sheridan advanced some of his infantry into Winchester. Cavalry sweeps thrust into the Shenandoah Valley ten to fifteen miles ahead of Sheridan's infantry in the valley and into Loudoun County on the east side of the Blue Ridge Mountains. During these sweeps, the cavalry destroyed the wheat and hay and drove off the cattle in the area south of Winchester and Berryville.

Sheridan's strength, Early's withdrawal, and the Yankee cavalry probes prompted Lee to send Early reinforcements: Kershaw's Infantry Division, two brigades of cavalry from Fitzhugh Lee's Cavalry Division, and Cutshaw's artillery battalion, all commanded by Richard Anderson. On August 14 Sheridan received a warning from Grant about these troops. Sheridan dispatched two brigades from Merritt's 1st Cavalry Division down the Front Royal Pike to investigate. On August 16 Kershaw's advancing troops encountered Union pickets at the Shenandoah River fords.

A short sharp action ensued. Kershaw's vanguard attacked the pickets, pushing them back to Guard Hill. There they ran into Thomas C. Devin's cavalry brigade (2nd Brigade, 1st Division), dismounted and in a strong defensive position. The Confederate attack stalled. Then other cavalrymen from Devin's brigade swept down. Attempting to rescue the situation, one of Kershaw's brigade commanders tried to flank the Union cavalry by crossing Crooked Run, a shallow creek. More Union cavalry struck while they were in mid-stream, routing the infantry. Nearly 300 Confederates along with two regimental standards were captured. Devin's brigade was soon joined by George A. Custer's brigade, but when Kershaw's main body came up, the Union cavalrymen took their captives and trophies, retreating up the Front Royal Pike to rejoin Sheridan.

Sheridan was falling back by then. Grant's message indicated that once the reinforcements joined, Early would have 40,000 men. It was a gross overestimation.

Robert E. Lee reacted to the Union buildup in the Shenandoah Valley by reinforcing Early. Fitzhugh Lee, a cousin of Robert E. Lee, commanded the two brigades of cavalry sent to the Shenandoah. Badly wounded at the Third Battle of Winchester, he missed the rest of the campaign. (AC)

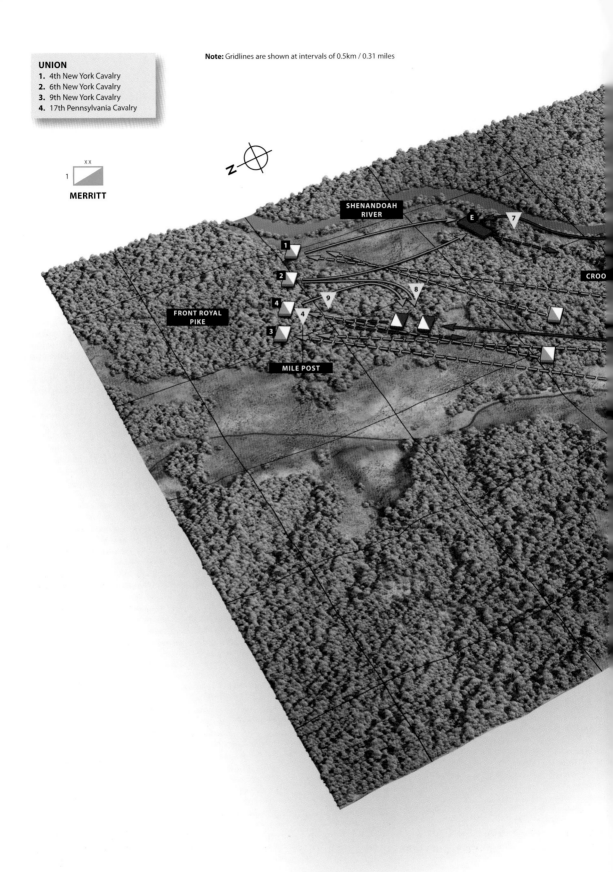

1 [XXX] ☒

ANDERSON

CONFEDERATE
A. 1st Virginia Cavalry
B. 2nd Virginia Cavalry
C. 3rd Virginia Cavalry
D. 4th Virginia Cavalry
E. Wofford's Brigade, Kershaw's Division
F. Johnston's Battery

SOUTH FORK OF THE SHENANDOAH RIVER

MANASSAS GAP RAILROAD

NORTH FORK OF THE SHENANDOAH RIVER

3. The 4th New York Cavalry countercharges, hitting Wickham's men in the flank, routing the Confederate horse and capturing one set of regimental colors.

4. The units from Devin's Brigade fall back to Mile Post, setting up a defensive line between the Shenandoah River and Crooked Run.

5. The 2nd Virginia Cavalry fords the Shenandoah downstream from the pike. During the fighting on the pike, the 2nd Virginia takes the heights between the Shenandoah River and the pike, dismounting and setting up a defensive perimeter.

6. Wofford's Brigade (from Kershaw's Division) fords the Shenandoah, flanking Devin's 2nd Brigade.

7. As Wofford's Brigade crosses Crooked Run, Devin sends the 4th New York Cavalry and two squadrons (battalions) of the 6th New York to attack. The cavalry charge catches the infantry crossing the creek, before they can form for battle. Wofford's men are pushed into the creek. During the struggle, Union forces capture 300 Confederate infantry and another regimental standard.

8. As Devin's cavalry strikes Wofford's men, Wickham personally leads a charge down the Front Royal Pike, to relieve Wofford.

▼ **EVENTS**

9. Devin countercharges with his reserves, again catching Wickham's cavalry in the flank, routing it back down the pike.

1. Anderson, his two divisions and a battalion of artillery are marching up the Front Royal Pike to Winchester when they unexpectedly encounter Union cavalry pickets from Devin's 2nd Brigade, 1st Cavalry Division guarding the crossings of the South Fork Shenandoah River.

10. The Confederates move artillery (Johnston's Battery) on Guard Hill, and begin bombarding Devin's forces. Although reinforced by the 1st Brigade of 1st Cavalry Division, commanded by George Custer, two unsupported cavalry brigades are no match for the two divisions. Having suffered 71 casualties, while capturing 480 prisoners and two regimental standards, Devin and Custer retreat back to Winchester.

2. At 2.00pm lead elements of the Virignia Cavalry units (from Wickham's Brigade) make contact with the 9th New York Cavalry, picketed on the crests on either side of the turnpike. Lead elements of Wickham's Brigade charge down the Front Royal Pike, attacking the Union troops.

THE BATTLE OF GUARD HILL, AUGUST 16

Guard Hill was one result of Lee and Early assuming Sheridan was yet another slow-moving and timid general, typical of those the Confederates often faced in the Eastern Theater. A classic meeting engagement, it resulted when reinforcements sent to Jubal Early stumbled upon two Union cavalry brigades conducting a reconnaissance in force.

Early's force never exceeded 20,000 effectives. Sheridan also received reports that at least two more infantry divisions, one from Anderson's I Corps, and one from A.P. Hill's III Corps, were being sent to the Shenandoah. In view of his orders for caution, Sheridan decided to wait for his reinforcements before challenging Early.

Receiving word of Sheridan's retreat, Early pushed north from Strasburg. He caught Sheridan's rearguard at Winchester on August 17—a brigade of infantry and Wilson's cavalry division. The Union line held until evening, when a massed attack by three Confederate infantry divisions broke them. The infantry brigade lost one-third of its force: 97 killed and 200 captured. Fifty Union cavalrymen were also taken. Hearing the fate of his rearguard, Sheridan had his army concentrate south of Charles Town.

Sensing weakness, Early sent both his corps and Anderson's Corps in pursuit. On August 21 Early caught the Union VI Corps on the road to Charles Town, near Summit Point, West Virginia. A short, sharp action occurred. VI Corps, aided by Wilson's 3rd Cavalry Division, held off Anderson's Corps, aided by Rodes's and Ramseur's infantry divisions. Meanwhile, Merritt's 1st Cavalry Division stalled and Wharton's Division advanced along the Berryville Pike. At dusk the Union army broke off, and retreated to Charles Town. Total casualties for both sides were perhaps 1,000. The 2nd Division of VI Corps suffered the heaviest losses: 260 killed and wounded.

Sheridan forted up at Halltown, while Early re-established his headquarters at Bunker Hill. After two weeks of fighting, both armies had returned to where they had started. The two armies were fighting different wars, however. Early wanted to interdict the Baltimore & Ohio Railroad. It ran from Harpers Ferry to Martinsburg, and from there to the Potomac River at Cherry Run, West Virginia. With his army camped outside of Halltown, it was impossible for the Union to use the Baltimore & Ohio Railroad. Even if Early only controlled the area around Bunker Hill, his cavalry could easily break the railroad with raids.

When news of reinforcements for Early reached Sheridan, who was under orders to behave cautiously, he fell back from Winchester to Harpers Ferry. Early pursued Sheridan, catching his rearguard at Summit Point. A brief skirmish resulted there. (AC)

Sheridan did not care about the railroad. His objective was Early's army. His movements centered on moving into a position where he could strike a decisive blow at his opponent. At this stage, under orders to proceed cautiously, Sheridan wanted to trap an isolated portion of the Army of the Valley, or force Early into an untenable position with the Confederates forced to fight at a disadvantage. This explained the thrusts south followed by withdrawals north, when Early proved too canny to be trapped.

Early spent three days probing the defenses of Halltown. Finally deciding it was too strong to attack, on August 25 Early left Anderson with Kershaw's Division and a division of cavalry to cover the town. He sent Lee's cavalry, less one regiment, to Williamsport, Maryland, while taking his remaining four divisions of infantry and his artillery towards Shepherdstown, West Virginia.

Early's stated goal was to again threaten Maryland and Pennsylvania, yet he never crossed the Potomac. Lee found the Williamsport crossings covered by William W. Averell's 2nd Cavalry Division. Early found his way contested by Merritt's and Wilson's divisions. However, these two cavalry divisions were no match for four infantry divisions. The Yankees were muscled aside, with Custer's brigade cut off by the Rebel advance. Custer's command escaped only by crossing the Potomac at Shepherdstown. Early did not follow.

Sheridan hoped Early would take the bait offered. Had Early crossed the Potomac, Sheridan had planned to cut off any retreat back south. Perhaps Early sensed the trap that crossing the deceptively unguarded Potomac would trigger.

Since Early declined the gambit, on August 26 Crook's infantry (with cavalry support) struck Anderson, taking the earthworks the Confederates had thrown up around Halltown. Crook had two further corps backing him up. Anderson, considerably weaker than Crook's forces, fell back to

During the first week of the campaign, Sheridan unleashed his cavalry on the lower valley. Cavalry foraging destroyed or carried off the crops and livestock south of Winchester and Berryville. This was a deliberate attempt to prevent Confederate forces from drawing rations from the region. (AC)

The action at Summit Point, August 21.

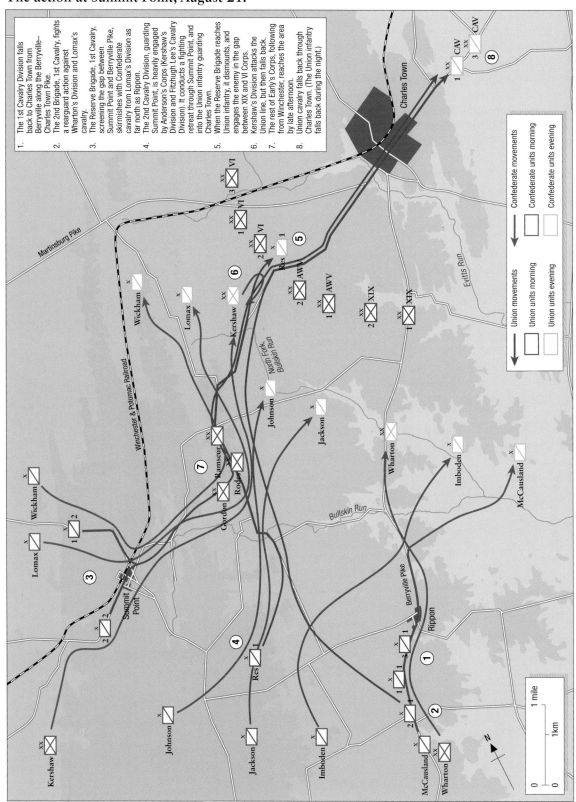

1. The 1st Cavalry Division falls back to Charles Town from Berryville along the Berryville–Charles Town Pike.
2. The 2nd Brigade, 1st Cavalry, fights a rearguard action against Wharton's Division and Lomax's cavalry.
3. The Reserve Brigade, 1st Cavalry, screening the gap between Summit Point and Berryville Pike, skirmishes with Confederate cavalry from Lomax's Division as far north as Rippon.
4. The 2nd Cavalry Division, guarding Summit Point, is heavily engaged by Anderson's Corps (Kershaw's Division and Fitzhugh Lee's Cavalry Division). It conducts a fighting retreat through Summit Point, and into the Union infantry guarding Charles Town.
5. When the Reserve Brigade reaches Union infantry, it dismounts, and engages the enemy in the gap between XIX and VI Corps.
6. Kershaw's Division attacks the Union line, but then falls back.
7. The rest of Early's Corps, following from Winchester, reaches the area by late afternoon.
8. Union cavalry falls back through Charles Town. (The Union infantry falls back during the night.)

Union movements →   **Confederate movements** →

Union units morning   Confederate units morning

Union units evening   Confederate units evening

0   1 mile

0   1km

Stephenson's Depot, northeast of Winchester. Early, realizing that he was again flanked, dropped back to Bunker Hill.

On August 28 Sheridan again pushed his infantry forward to Charles Town, Averell's division to Martinsburg, Wilson's to Shepherdstown, and Merritt's to Leetown.

Merritt found Confederate cavalry in Leetown, and attacked. A running engagement followed. The Confederates skedaddled through Smithfield and across the Opequon Creek with Merritt's division, sabers drawn, in pursuit. That night, Merritt encamped in Smithfield.

Early sent Rodes's Division to drive Averell out of Martinsburg. He sent two other infantry divisions to attack Merritt. Averell prudently fell back to Falling Waters, on the Potomac. Merritt was chased out of Smithfield, but, reinforced by the 3rd Division of VI Corps, counterattacked and retook the town. The following day, August 30, Wilson's division joined these forces, and continued pushing the Confederates south. By August 31 Sheridan had his three infantry corps back in a line between Clifton and Berryville. By September 3 they were anchored in a line with VI Corps at Clifton, the Army of West Virginia in Berryville, XIX Corps between these two, and Merritt and Wilson's cavalry divisions covering the flanks.

While Early and Sheridan had danced between Harpers Ferry and Winchester, events outside the theater were affecting the Shenandoah campaign. On September 2 Sherman captured Atlanta. Word of the victory reached Sheridan the next day. The victory unleashed Sheridan, allowing him to act more aggressively.

Simultaneously, Lee's situation at Petersburg was deteriorating. Lee desperately needed more troops, and had nothing in reserve. He believed Early had enough troops to contain Sheridan and decided to recall some of the reinforcements he had sent to the valley in early August. On August 31 Anderson, along with Kershaw's Division, had withdrawn to Winchester, in preparation for returning to Petersburg. Three days later, on September 3, this division started its march back to Lee, crossing the Blue Ridge Mountains through Snicker's Gap via Berryville.

One hour before sunset, Kershaw's Division marched right into the Army of West Virginia encamped in Berryville. Mutual surprise resulted in a confused skirmish. Kershaw's men scattered the Union pickets, but were thrown back as the Union reacted. Before darkness ended that day's battle, Crook suffered 166 casualties and Anderson had 60 men taken prisoner. Fortunately for the outnumbered Anderson, darkness concealed his vulnerable baggage trains, and Sheridan's two available cavalry divisions were on a scout somewhere between Millwood and Front Royal.

Early hurried to Anderson's relief with Rodes's, Ramseur's, and Breckinridge's divisions. When Early arrived on September 4, he found Kershaw in an extended skirmish line and the Army of West Virginia in front of Kershaw. Early deployed one division to Kershaw's left. The other two he swung further to the left in an attempt to flank Sheridan on the right. As Early advanced, he realized he was moving on Sheridan's center, not the flank. Sheridan's army was entrenched from Berryville to Summit Point.

Unwilling to assault a fortified line, outnumbered, and recognizing he would be flanked by Sheridan's cavalry if he stood his ground, Early fell back. He sent Anderson's trains to Winchester, conducting a fighting retreat back across Opequon Creek, harried by the two returning Union cavalry divisions. Total casualties for both sides on the two days of the Battle of Berryville were about 600, split more or less evenly between Union and Confederate.

To add to Confederate frustration, on September 5 they discovered Sheridan's remaining cavalry division (Averell's 2nd) chasing the Confederate cavalry left to cover the Martinsburg road back to Winchester. Rodes's Division, by then back at Stephenson's Depot, deployed and pushed Averell back to Bunker Hill.

Over the next ten days the two armies remained in position. Sheridan's Army of the Shenandoah held the line between Summit Point and Berryville. Early's Army of the Valley concentrated in an arc around Winchester. Sheridan, freed from his early instructions to avoid defeat, launched a series of probes along the Opequon Creek, testing Early's lines for weaknesses.

At first these skirmishes were conducted solely by Union cavalry, and were fought in regimental and brigade strengths. On September 5, the 2nd Brigade of Averell's cavalry division skirmished near Stephenson's Depot. On September 7th the 2nd Brigade of Wilson's cavalry division probed Brucetown and Winchester. Then individual Union infantry regiments began participating. On September 8 the 176th New York tested the Confederates near Berryville.

This was followed by cavalry and infantry regiments acting jointly. On September 13 the 1st Brigade of Wilson's division struck Abrams Creek near Winchester, the 1st and 2nd brigades of 2nd Division, VI Corps conducted a demonstration at Gilbert's Ford on Opequon Creek, and the 1st and Reserve brigades of Merritt's 1st Cavalry Division ran a similar show of force at Opequon Creek's Locke's Ford.

For all the sound and fury by Sheridan's army, there was very little movement. Sheridan did not seem to be trying to move the Confederates so much as probing them. Grant began losing patience with his protégé. He began prodding Sheridan to do something, especially after September 3, when word of Sherman's capture of Atlanta reached Virginia. Grant had given Sheridan a big slice of Union manpower and Grant wanted something more than thrust and parry with Early. Early began feeling he had gained Sheridan's measure, and was becoming convinced that Sheridan's measure

August 21 ended with the Army of the Shenandoah falling back through Charles Town and stopping outside Halltown, just west of Harpers Ferry. Two weeks after the campaign started, Sheridan's army was virtually back where it had started. (AC)

was coming up short. Early's experiences over the last month led him to peg Sheridan as yet another plodding Union general.

One thing was certain. Early could safely return some of Lee's reinforcements to the Army of Northern Virginia. Sheridan's advance to the Berryville–Summit Point line ten days earlier startled Early into hanging on to these soldiers. Ten days of Union relative immobility had convinced Early that he could hang on with fewer troops.

On September 14 Anderson departed Winchester with Kershaw's Division and Cutshaw's Artillery Battalion. He left Fitzhugh Lee's Cavalry Division with Early. This time, to avoid again tangling with the Yankees, Anderson took a more southerly route. He headed off to Newtown. From there he would march to Front Royal and through the Chester Gap. It was a roundabout route, well away from the front.

There was a method to Sheridan's actions in those first two weeks of September. The apparently purposeless probing was Sheridan's method of shaking down his troops. He was getting to know them; they were getting to know him. More than that, Sheridan was testing a new tactical doctrine: combined operations.

While cavalry and infantry played useful roles throughout the Civil War, the two branches tended to act independently. Cavalry raided; it also scouted out the location of the enemy army's main body, or prevented the enemy's cavalry from finding the location of their main body. Once the two armies met, the cavalry generally fell back and let the infantry go to work. Even flanking the enemy, as at Chancellorsville, was typically done by infantry.

Sheridan was experimenting with integrating the actions of his cavalry and his infantry. He wanted to use his men in a new way. During battles, the infantry would pin down the Confederate forces. Then the cavalry, with its superior mobility, would sweep around, cut off the enemy's retreat routes, and break them into pockets. The trapped forces would then be crushed between the infantry and the cavalry. Sheridan's goal was not just victory; it was annihilation. All he needed was the right moment to strike. When reports began reaching Sheridan about Anderson's departure, he knew that moment had arrived.

Finding Sheridan's Halltown entrenchments too strong, Early attempted another raid across the Potomac. Sheridan sent cavalry to cover the Potomac River crossings. Early dislodged the Union cavalry and reached the Potomac, but chose to remain on the river's south bank, unwilling to risk getting trapped in Maryland by Sheridan. (AC)

CAMPAIGN IN THE SHENANDOAH VALLEY—THE FEDERAL FORCES FALLING BACK THROUGH CHARLESTOWN, AUGUST 21st, 1864.

MEETING THE UNION PICKET LINE AT BERRYVILLE (PP. 50–51)

In the first month of Sheridan's Shenandoah Campaign, Kershaw's Division never seemed to have a smooth passage entering or leaving the valley. They had to fight their way in when they encountered a Yankee cavalry division on their entrance on August 16. Then, as they tried to leave the valley two weeks later, they ran into another Union outfit, this time on the Berryville Pike.

It seemed that Early had things in hand when Anderson, along with Kershaw's Division and Cutshaw's Artillery Battalion, was ordered back to Petersburg by Robert E. Lee. They left Winchester on September 3, planning a direct march through Snicker's Gap along the Berryville Pike. They expected a fast march through friendly territory. Sheridan's infantry, the Confederates believed, were at Charles Town, and Sheridan's cavalry was north of that, sparring with the rest of Early's army along the route of the Baltimore & Ohio Railroad.

They were working on old news. That morning Sheridan had moved south. He was in the process of reoccupying the lines he held in August that ran from Berryville to Summit Point. As a result, an hour before sunset Kershaw's advance guard marched smack into the 1st Division of Crook's Army of West Virginia one mile northwest of Berryville.

The encounter was a surprise for both sides. Kershaw's Division was in march formation. Their baggage train was with them.

Crook's men were setting up camp for the night. It is hard to say which side was more taken aback.

Kershaw, worried about his vulnerable train, acted first. He sent his men against the Union pickets. As shown in this illustration, Kershaw's infantrymen (1) discarded their packs and formed into line. The lead companies deployed as skirmishers (2). The men following formed into battle line (3).

Crook's picket line (4), attacked by Kershaw's formed infantry, scattered. They fell back one-half mile to their main battle line, on a hill shielding the divisional encampment. There the Confederate advance stopped. A confused melee broke out in the evening twilight. Darkness brought an eventual end to the fighting. Darkness also gave Kershaw and Anderson the chance to withdraw the baggage train, at risk from a Union advance.

That evening's action was indecisive, as measured by the casualty count. Crook's forces took 167 casualties: 24 dead, 124 wounded, and 19 missing. Kershaw had 60 men taken prisoner. It had significant long-term consequences, however. The battle delayed Kershaw's transfer back to the Army of Northern Virginia. His troops returned to Winchester, where they spent ten days before finally departing the valley. More importantly, it signaled a new, more aggressive Phil Sheridan.

THE THIRD BATTLE OF WINCHESTER, SEPTEMBER 15–19

Among the things Sheridan had done since occupying the line between Clifton and Berryville was to organize a group of scouts. These men, recruited from the army at large, volunteered to scout behind Confederate lines in Confederate uniforms. They were to mingle with the civilian population, and extract information about the enemy position and strength. While organized into a provisional battalion, these men probably never exceeded company strength—100 men.

This was not without risk to these volunteers. If caught while in enemy uniform, they could expect summary execution. Nor was it without precedent. Benjamin Grierson owed much of his success in his cavalry raid through Mississippi in May 1863 to a similar set of scouts, organized by a sergeant in one of his cavalry regiments.

Sheridan's scouts brought word of Anderson's September 14 departure. They also found evidence that Early had left Winchester, but lacked proof. Sheridan wanted confirmation of Anderson's departure and Early's location.

What happened next can be likened to something out of a boy's adventure novel. Sheridan asked Crook, familiar with the valley, if Crook knew anyone in Winchester loyal to the Union willing to send intelligence about Confederate dispositions and produce reliable observations. Crook recommended Rebecca Wright, whom he had met before the Battle of Kernstown. A Quaker and teacher at a small private school, she opposed slavery.

The Third Battle of Winchester opened with Wilson's 3rd Cavalry Division capturing the Confederate earthworks at Opequon Creek. This allowed the 3rd Division of VI Corps, commanded by James B. Ricketts, to attack Ramseur's Division through the rolling woods west of Opequon Creek. (AC)

To reach her, Sheridan turned to his scouts. They knew of an old black man, sympathetic to the Union, who lived in Millwood. He had a pass to travel to Winchester three times a week to sell vegetables. He knew Wright and agreed to serve as messenger. On September 16 he walked into her classroom, handing her a message that read:

September 15, 1864.
I learn from Major-General Crook that you are a loyal lady, and still love the old flag. Can you inform me of the position of Early's forces, the number of divisions in his army, and the strength of any or all of them, and his probable or reported intentions? Have any more troops arrived from Richmond, or are any more coming, or reported to be coming?
    You can trust the bearer.
    I am, very respectfully, your most obedient servant,
    P. H. SHERIDAN, Major-General Commanding.

On the evening of September 16, Sheridan received her response:

I have no communication whatever with the rebels, but will tell you what I know. The division of General Kershaw, and Cutshaw's artillery, twelve guns and men, General Anderson commanding, have been sent away, and no more are expected, as they cannot be spared from Richmond. I do not know how the troops are situated, but the force is much smaller than represented. I will take pleasure hereafter in learning all I can of their strength and position, and the bearer may call again.

That was enough. Sheridan began planning an attack on Newtown, southwest of Winchester. As the planning went forward, Sheridan was called away to a meeting with Grant at Charles Town, West Virginia. Grant, frustrated by Sheridan's inactivity over the last two weeks, wanted to prod his subordinate into action. Word of Anderson's departure and Sheridan's planned attack satisfied Grant. He agreed with Sheridan's assessment that the attack should be delayed a few days to ensure Anderson's men were too far away to interfere.

By late morning on September 19, XIX Corps was deployed to the right of VI Corps. Just before noon, XIX Corps launched an attack against Gordon's Division, advancing across an open field to reach the Confederate positions. (AC)

As for Early, he was lulled by Sheridan's passivity and worried about reports that the Baltimore & Ohio Railroad was being repaired. The day after Rebecca Wright received Sheridan's letter, Early marched Rodes's and Gordon's divisions and the bulk of his cavalry back to Bunker Hill. He left Ramseur's Division in Winchester guarding the Berryville Pike, and Wharton (who had succeeded John C. Breckinridge in command of that infantry division) at Stephenson's Depot. Early left them a brigade of cavalry for screening.

Early chased Averell out of Bunker Hill that evening. The next day Early sent Gordon's Division and Lomax's Cavalry to Martinsburg in pursuit of Averell. He also ordered Rodes back to Stephenson's Depot. On the evening of September 18 (the night before the Third Battle of Winchester) the Army of the Valley was scattered. The cavalry was at Martinsburg. Gordon was at Bunker Hill. Rodes, with Braxton's Artillery Battalion, was marching to Stephenson's Depot. Wharton, with King's Artillery Battalion, was at Stephenson's Depot, and Ramseur, with Nelson's Artillery Battalion, was covering the approach from Berryville.

On September 18 Sheridan, preparing a move to Newtown, received word from Averell that he had been attacked by two infantry divisions. Sheridan realized this meant Winchester was lightly guarded. Sheridan had what he wanted since taking command: the opportunity to overwhelm part of Early's army, destroying it in detail. At a minimum a quick thrust to Winchester would snag Early's supply train. Sheridan altered his marching plan.

Torbert, with Merritt's 1st Cavalry, was to move from Summit Point to Stephenson's Depot. There he would meet Averell's 2nd Cavalry, which would move from Darksville. Wilson's 3rd Cavalry would move down the Berryville Pike and capture the Opequon crossings. The cavalry would be followed by the VI and XIX corps, in that order. Finally, in reserve, the Army of West Virginia would follow. The movement would occur during the night of September 18/19.

Speed was essential. Sheridan knew that once Early discovered the Army of the Shenandoah was moving, Early would concentrate his forces. To get his army to Winchester from Berryville, Sheridan needed to move three infantry corps and a cavalry division—roughly 33,000 men—down a single road. Three miles from Berryville, the Berryville Pike passed through a steep and narrow gorge where it crossed Limestone Ridge. Anticipating the bottleneck, Sheridan ordered: "All regimental and other wagons that will inconvenience the quick movement of the troops will be parked at Summit Point with the supply train, and sent under guard to Harpers Ferry."

The attack started as planned. Wilson's cavalry division pushed through first, followed closely by Horatio Wright's VI Corps. The cavalry struck the outlying Confederate earthworks guarding the crossing of Opequon Creek at dawn, easily taking them. It dismounted, defending the crossing against a determined counterattack by Ramseur's men backed by artillery. The repeating breechloaders stopped the Confederate infantry. VI Corps followed, deploying in the rolling terrain past the cavalry. By 9.00am, four hours after Wilson's cavalry first attacked, VI Corps was moving against Ramseur.

Then Sheridan's plans started falling apart. Rodes's Division rushed to aid Ramseur, with Gordon's men right behind them. By 10.00am, instead of facing Ramseur's lone division, Wright was facing three infantry divisions.

(Early held his fourth infanty division, Wharton's, along with the bulk of his cavalry at Stephenson's Depot.) Worse, VI Corps was facing the Confederates unsupported. Once Wright had passed the cavalry, Wilson remounted and moved his men to the left to flank the Confederates.

XIX Corps and the Army of West Virginia were absent. They were still struggling to cross Limestone Ridge. Ignoring orders, Wright brought his trains behind his infantry. The Berryville Pike was jammed with wagons, and XIX Corps was corked behind these wagons. Although the troops were snaking around the wagons, their progress was achingly slow. It was not until Sheridan arrived, investigating the delay, that progress resumed. A furious Sheridan ordered the train run into the ditches. It was not until 11.00am that XIX Corps arrived at the battlefield.

By then, Sheridan's original plan was dead. The Confederates had stitched together a line. Ramseur covered both sides of the Berryville Pike. Rodes was to Ramseur's left, in a stand of woods. Gordon was deployed to Rodes's left, with his flank anchored on Redbud Run, a shallow creek. Some Confederate cavalry was in front of him. Beyond Redbud Run, Gordon depended on Wharton's Division and Fitzhugh Lee's cavalry to shield him.

Sheridan hastily improvised a new attack plan. He deployed XIX Corps to the right of VI Corps, and pushed both corps forward, holding one division of VI Corps in reserve. Meanwhile, he ordered Wilson down the Senseny Road, south of the Berryville Pike. Wilson was to swing south of Winchester to cut off Early's retreat. Originally, Sheridan intended Crook to join Wilson. Instead he ordered Crook to the right of XIX Corps, north of Redbud Run.

When the two Union corps attacked, a gap developed between VI Corps and XIX Corps. A fresh brigade from Rodes's Division arrived just as the gap appeared, and promptly exploited it, charging in. They were joined by the rest of Rodes's Division and Gordon's Division. A short, fierce fight developed. The two Yankee divisions at the corps' boundary were pushed back. Robert Rodes fell mortally wounded during the assault.

The Confederate charge opened a gap in their lines. The reserve division, 1st Division from VI Corps, led by Brigadier-General David Russell, counterattacked. They struck the flanks of the Confederates as Rodes's and Gordon's men wheeled VI Corps to the right and XIX Corps to the left. The Confederate infantry was pushed back to their original position. This assault cost the Union a divisional commander. Russell was struck by a shell fragment while leading the attack. By then it was well past noon.

Brigadier-General David A. Russell was Philip Sheridan's friend and confidant. The friendship had been forged in the Pacific Northwest, when Russell was Sheridan's superior, and survived the change in relationship. Russell's division, held in reserve, launched a critical counterattack that stopped a Confederate advance. (AC)

Crook's corps was now in position, and the cavalry had arrived. Alfred Torbert, with two divisions of cavalry, had been pushing down from the north. This 7,000-strong force had faced the 2,000 infantrymen in Wharton's Division, and 1,500 cavalrymen in Lee's Division. By 1.00pm they were at Stephenson's Depot, having shoved the Confederate forces opposing them back. By 3.00pm they were along Redbud Run, with Crook to their left.

The Confederate line was now pushed into an L-shape. Gordon's Division held the angle, while Rodes's Division and Ramseur's Division held the eastern line of the L. All three divisions were exhausted by the day's fighting. To the left of Gordon, only Patton's Brigade of Wharton's Division and part of Lee's cavalry held the northern leg. Early, realizing he was losing, had been sending his trains out of Winchester, and was sending his cavalry south of Winchester, to keep a line of retreat open.

It was a wise precaution. Wilson's cavalry had been driving towards the junction of the Front Royal Pike and Millwood Pike all afternoon. Lomax's cavalry had been fighting a delaying action but were steadily being pushed back. If Lomax failed to hold, Early would be trapped in Winchester with Union forces on three sides, and the Great North Mountains on the remaining side. Early reinforced Lomax with whatever cavalry was available.

At 4.30pm Sheridan launched a final attack. VI Corps and XIX Corps pinned the eastern leg of the Confederate line. The fresh infantry of Crook's Army of West Virginia slammed into Gordon's share of the northern leg. Finally, at 5.00pm Torbert launched two divisions of cavalry, led by George Custer's brigade, into a charge against the lightly held Confederate left.

At first the Confederates fell back in good order, bringing their artillery with them. They had fought stubbornly all day, giving as good as they got. Early, receiving an erroneous report that the Yankees were breaking through on his right, ordered a general retreat. In reality, the "advancing" Yankees were actually Ramseur's Division, falling back in formation.

The cavalry charge finished the Army of the Valley. It was unprecedented in the Civil War. The sight of 7,000 saber-waving cavalrymen riding down on them from an unexpected direction caused panic. They began to run. At first they ran for Winchester, seeking shelter in the buildings of the town. Once in Winchester, they kept going. The retreat soon turned into a rout.

The traffic jam at Limestone Ridge delayed Crook's Army of West Virginia. They did not deploy until afternoon, only launching their attack at 3.30pm. Their charge against the northern line of Early's army proved decisive to the ultimate Union victory. (AC)

The Third Battle of Winchester (or Opequon), 6.00am–11.00am.

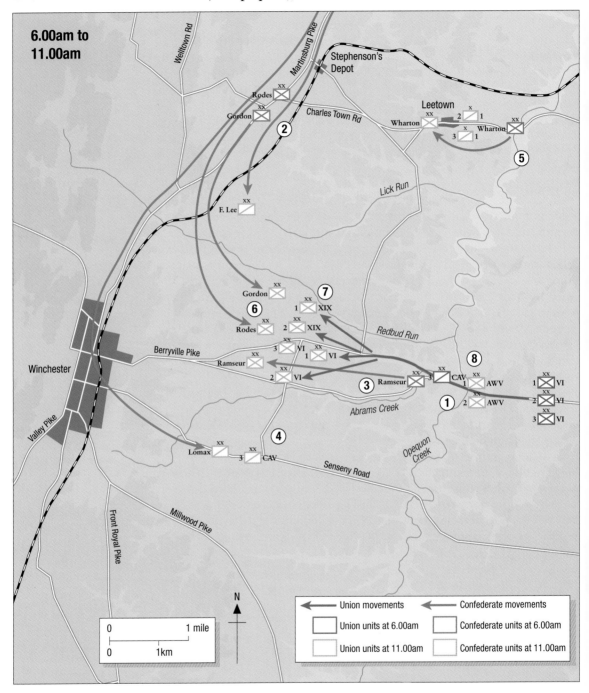

1. 6.00am: US 3rd Cavalry captures the Opequon Creek crossing.
2. 7.00am: Early sends Rodes's and Gordon's divisions to help Ramseur; he also sends Wharton's Division and cavalry to cover the Opequon crossing east of Leetown.
3. 9.00am: VI Corps deploys against Ramseur's Division.
4. 10.00am: 3rd Cavalry is sent to cut the roads south of Winchester.
5. 10.00am: Elements of the 1st Cavalry Division attack Wharton, driving the Confederates back to Leetown.
6. 10.00am: Rodes and Gordon join Ramseur. VI Corps is fighting three divisions unaided.
7. 11.00am: XIX Corps deploys to the right of VI Corps.
8. 11.00am: Crook's Corps arrives at the Opequon crossing and is directed north of Redbud Run.

The Third Battle of Winchester (or Opequon), 3.00pm–5.00pm.

3.00pm–5.00pm.

9. 11.00am to 3.00pm: VI and XIX Corps push Ramseur's, Rodes's, and Gordon's divisions back.
10. 11.00am to 3.00pm: 2nd Cavalry Division and rest of 1st Cavalry Division arrive via the Martinsburg Pike, reuniting with the 1st Cavalry brigades and driving Wharton and Fitzhugh Lee's divisions towards Winchester.
11. 11.00am to 3.00pm: 3rd Cavalry skirmishes with Lomax's cavalry along the Senseny Road.
12. 3.00pm: Crook's divisions establish positions north of Redbud Run flanking the Confederates facing the VI and XIX corps.
13. 4.30pm: General attack by Union infantry corps.
14. 5.00pm: Final Confederate defensive position at Winchester.
15. 5.00pm: 1st and 2nd Cavalry divisions charge, routing the Confederate line.
16. 5.00pm to 7.00pm: Lomax's cavalry stops the 3rd Cavalry on the Front Royal Pike.
17. 5.00pm to 7.00pm: The Army of the Valley escapes down Valley Pike.

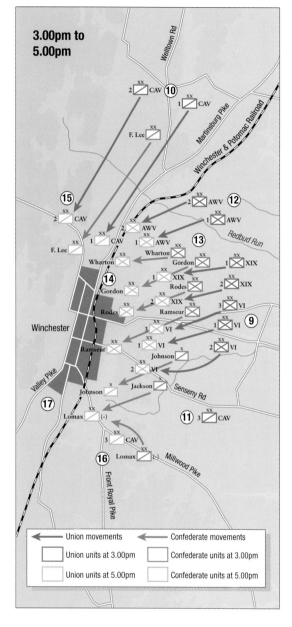

The men ignored their officers, who were yelling at them to stand. George Patton, grandfather and namesake of the World War II armor leader, commanded a brigade in Wharton's Division. He tried to rally his crumbling brigade in the streets of Winchester. He was killed by a Union sniper.

Pro-Confederate ladies in Winchester stood on their porches, and shouted at the fleeing men, trying to shame them into fighting. They were ignored. Fanny Gordon, Major-General John Gordon's wife, ran into streets attempting to rally the army. She was discovered there by her husband, leading a rearguard. He ordered her back to shelter. With the help of some men in his command, she harnessed her carriage and rode out of town with her six-year-old son, a black servant, and two wounded officers.

Suddenly, it was over. Early's army was out of Winchester, and Sheridan's army was in possession. It was the 73rd, and last, time Winchester would change hands during the Civil War. Sheridan rode into the town. When he wanted to write a telegraph to Grant, Crook took him to Rebecca Wright's home. Sheridan thanked her for her assistance, and wrote the telegraph in her schoolroom.

The Army of the Valley had taken a licking. They lost nearly 1,800 killed and wounded. Between 1,800 and 2,000 men had been taken prisoner. Among the dead were Rodes and Patton. Also dead was Archibald Godwin, who commanded a brigade in Ramseur's Division. Fizhugh Lee was badly wounded. So was Zebulon York, who commanded a brigade in Gordon's Division. Five guns and nine regimental standards had been lost.

Yet it could have been much worse. Early's decision to re-concentrate and his prompt action in doing so prevented the annihilation of Ramseur's Division. It also prevented his army from being trapped. The unexpected appearance of Rodes and Gordon had forced Sheridan to send Crook to his right flank instead of his left. While Crook's presence there contributed to the ultimate

The Valley Turnpike (or Valley Pike) was the main road for the Shenandoah Valley, virtually the only route capable of reliably moving heavy wagons and cannon at reasonable speeds. Most of the major battles in the Shenandoah were fought along its length, generally at choke points such as Fisher's Hill. (AC)

Confederate collapse, it weakened Sheridan's encirclement. By 5.00pm Wilson's Division controlled only one of the three remaining roads out of Winchester. It lacked the strength to take the other two until after the Confederates escaped, even after being reinforced by VI and XIX corps. Early's recognition that he was losing, and his prompt evacuation of his trains and wounded, also preserved his army's ability to fight.

Despite the infantry rout at the battle's end, he kept most of his artillery and was able to reorganize his remaining forces into a fighting force the next day.

Union casualties were even heavier than those of the Confederacy. The Army of the Shenandoah lost 4,300 men killed and wounded, including Brigadier-General David Russell killed, and five brigade and divisional commanders badly wounded. Nearly 600 men were missing, although some of the missing returned over the next few days.

Regardless, it was a major Union victory. The men and leaders Early lost were irreplaceable. Union control of the lower Shenandoah Valley was undisputed. Abraham Lincoln had received another boost to his re-election campaign. It also marked the first time in the Civil War that cavalry had been used in conjunction with infantry to decide a battle.

Sheridan was the toast of the North. The victory vindicated Grant's choice of Sheridan, one for which Grant had been receiving increasing criticism. Sheridan received a personal note of thanks from Abraham Lincoln, and a more tangible reward from Secretary of War Edwin Stanton in the form of a

The Third Battle of Winchester cost the Army of the Valley nearly 1,800 casualties. Most of the dead were left on the battlefield to be recovered and buried by the Union army that night and on the following day. Union parties discovered one slain Confederate soldier still attended by his faithful dog, guarding his dead master's body. (AC)

promotion. While Sheridan had held the brevet rank of brigadier-general since July 1862, this was a temporary rank. After Winchester, Stanton made Sheridan a brigadier-general in the regular army, making Sheridan's star permanent.

FISHER'S HILL, SEPTEMBER 20–23

Although Early's army was down, it was far from out. The Third Battle of Winchester (or, as Sheridan preferred calling it, Opequon Creek) may have cost the Army of the Valley 20–25 percent of its strength, but the core of Early's army remained. The moment of panic at the battle's end quickly passed, and never affected most of the army. Ramseur's, Rodes's, and most of Gordon's divisions withdrew in good order.

The artillery lost had been from artillery batteries supporting Wharton's and Lee's divisions, the two units hardest hit during the battle. Even there the losses had not resulted from panic. Rather, the horses pulling them had been killed, and the swift pace of the Union advance swallowed the guns before new teams could replace the losses.

Instead of retiring to the upper valley, and falling back to New Market or even Staunton, Early chose to reoccupy prepared fortifications at Fisher's Hill. The latter, just south of Strasburg, formed a natural strong point. It marks the northern tip of the Massanutten mountain chain, a spot where the main valley narrows from twelve miles to four miles.

Tumbling Run, a creek that skirts the northern flanks of the ridge, served as a natural moat. Anchored by the North Fork of the Shenandoah River on the east, the position commands both the Valley Pike and the Manassas Gap Railroad. The Union could not move around this position, and had to take it to gain access to the upper valley. Early originally fortified this position in mid-August.

Once at Fisher's Hill, Early reorganized his army. In addition to the senior officers he had lost at Winchester, he was also losing the services of Major-General John Breckinridge, who was reassigned to southwest Virginia. Breckinridge, more senior than Early, had willingly served under Early, acting as a corps commander. As a result of the losses, Major-General Stephen Ramseur took command of Rodes's Division and Brigadier-General John Pegram took command of Ramseur's Division. These divisions took the names of their new

Massanutten Mountain brooded over the Confederate position at Fisher's Hill. It anchored the Confederate right, and provided a platform from which to observe all Union movement. (LOC)

commanders. William Wickham superseded the injured Fizhugh Lee to command Lee's Cavalry Division, although it was still called Lee's Division.

Early's fortifications were built to accommodate the five infantry divisions he had a month previously, not the four understrength divisions left after the Third Battle of Winchester. Additionally, to hold Fisher's Hill he had to guard against a Union cavalry sweep in his rear through the Luray Valley. This forced him to detach Lee's Division to cover Millford. That left only Lomax's Division, his other cavalry division remaining. To completely fill the Fisher's Hill fortifications, Early was forced to dismount the division to occupy the entrenchments on the line's left flank. Thus he lacked a mobile reserve, should Sheridan's men make a breakthrough.

It was a gamble Early was prepared to take. Fisher's Hill offered the best geographic position between New Market and Winchester. It could be easily supplied from the region immediately south of it, and the Valley Pike and Middle Road offered easy access to the Confederate lines. Early lacked the infantry to hold the full line, but reinforcements were coming. Kershaw's Division and Cutshaw's Artillery had reversed course and were marching back to Early. In addition, Lee was sending the remaining brigade of Lee's Division commanded by Thomas Rosser. They started for the Shenandoah on September 20. Once Kershaw returned, the manpower crisis would ease and he could pull the cavalry out of the lines. Given the stately progress of Sheridan's army prior to Winchester, Early thought he could reasonably assume Kershaw had time to return before the next battle.

Early was still underestimating Sheridan. Sheridan was not passively waiting at Winchester; he was following Early. At sunrise on September 20, Sheridan was already marching up the valley on the Valley Pike. Sheridan had sent his cavalry ahead on roads leading south out of Winchester. Merritt's 1st Cavalry Division was on the Valley Pike. Averell's 2nd Cavalry Division took the Cedar Creek Grade Road and the Middle Road until they reached Back Road, and pushed to the south on that. Wilson's 3rd Cavalry Division scouted down the Front Royal Pike. Merritt was followed by the rest of the Army of the Shenandoah. VI Corps deployed to the east of the Valley Pike, XIX Corps to the west, and Crook's corps-sized Army of West Virginia brought up the rear.

It did not take long for Merritt's cavalry to cover the 28 miles (45km) from Winchester to Early's advance positions on Fisher's Hill. Having made contact, the cavalrymen made no attempt to dislodge Early. Instead, messengers were sent to Sheridan, and the cavalry waited for the arrival of the infantry.

The Union cavalry charge, led by George A. Custer's Wolverine Brigade, against the Confederate left proved to be the blow that shattered the Rebel army at Winchester. The resulting Confederate retreat soon degenerated into a rout. (LOC)

The Battle of Fisher's Hill, September 21–22.

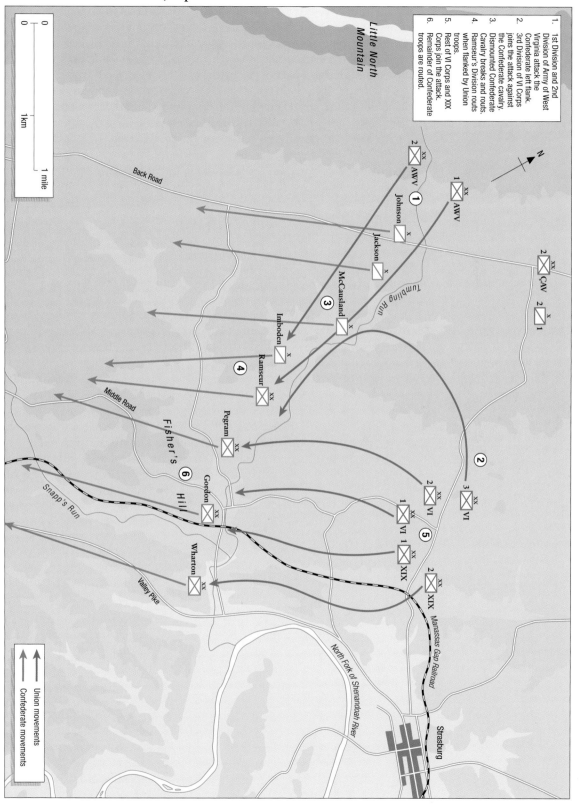

1. 1st Division and 2nd Division of Army of West Virginia attack the Confederate left flank.
2. 3rd Division of VI Corps joins the attack against the Confederate cavalry.
3. Dismounted Confederate Cavalry breaks and routs.
4. Ramseur's Division routs when flanked by Union troops.
5. Rest of VI Corps and XIX Corps join the attack.
6. Remainder of Confederate troops are routed.

Union movements
Confederate movements

The two lead corps arrived by mid-afternoon on September 20. They deployed on the heights west of Strasburg, with VI Corps on the right flank and XIX Corps to the left. XIX Corps extended its lines past the Front Royal Pike, almost to the Shenandoah River. By nightfall, Union pickets from XIX Corps held the northern streets of Strasburg, while Confederate pickets occupied the southern part of the town.

Crook's Corps was halted well back in heavy timber behind Cedar Creek, to the left of VI Corps and concealed by this unit. Once the infantry displaced the positions Merritt's cavalry had held, Sheridan pulled the division back, and then sent it to join Averell's division on Back Road. The two sides then settled in for the night, with no further action that day.

Sheridan spent September 21 positioning his infantry and scouting Early's position. The Confederate pickets were driven out of Strasburg, and the Confederate skirmishers back to the Fisher's Hill fortifications. Sheridan rode the length of the line, noting the ground.

A few tentative probes were made. Wright sent three regiments from his VI Corps to seize a hill north of Tumbling Run, directly across from the Confederate lines. A Confederate counterattack threw this back. Wright reinforced the attack with another brigade, and the hill was carried. Once taken, pioneers set up artillery positions on the hill.

Early's army spent the day strengthening his fortifications. They set up abatises, rows of tree branches with the ends sharpened and pointing outward. These were intended to slow an advancing attacker, giving the defenders more time to shoot them down in the open. They also built earth and stone ramparts to further protect their positions. As the sun set, they were prepared for the assault that would surely come the next day—an assault most believed would come across Tumbling Run.

Sheridan's forces did eventually come from the expected direction; however, the assault was the closing curtain rather than the opening act. Sheridan had previously commanded troops which successfully carried a strongly fortified Confederate line after attacking uphill. At Chattanooga his division changed a demonstration against the Confederate entrenchments atop Missionary Ridge into a charge that routed the Confederate center. He did not wish to attempt a duplicate of that unlikely result, however.

Sheridan's reconnaissance on September 21 showed Early's right flank was solidly anchored. Early's left flank was vulnerable, though, so Sheridan spent the day shifting his two visible corps slightly to the right. He moved XIX Corps opposite Wharton's and Gordon's divisions, while

Some of the 1,100 Confederates taken prisoner at Fisher's Hill are shown here, under guard, awaiting transportation to prisoner of war camps. (LOC)

Wright's VI Corps faced Ramseur's and Pegram's divisions. To the right of VI Corps was Averell's cavalry.

Sheridan also sent two brigades of the 1st Cavalry Division to join Wilson's 3rd Cavalry Division. Wilson had met the badly outnumbered cavalry of Lee's Division on the Front Royal Pike and pushed them back six miles (10km) up the Luray Valley. Sheridan reinforced Wilson to provide enough strength to cut off Early's eastern retreat routes, should Sheridan's attack on Fisher's Hill dislodge the Confederates. As for the western roads, Sheridan planned to send Averell to take the Valley Pike behind Early. With luck, Sheridan could pocket the Army of the Valley over the next two days.

Instead of a straight frontal assault, Sheridan planned to turn Early's left flank. He sent Crook's corps on a wide march around the Confederate left flank, with instructions to attack once they were in position. While demonstrations by VI and XIX corps fixed the attentions of the Confederates, Crook's men quietly slipped around the left flank of the Confederate lines. Using terrain and timber to shield the movement from a Confederate signal station on Three Top Mountain, five-and-a-half miles (9km) away, and on Round Hill, three miles (5km) away, the Union troops reached their positions undetected.

Early would later claim that the Union demonstrations convinced him that Fisher's Hill could not be held, and that he ordered preparations for a nighttime retreat. He never got the chance. At 4.00pm on September 22 his forces were still in their fortifications. After that, Early's plans became irrelevant. Crook's corps rolled out from Little North Mountain and onto the flank of Lomax's dismounted cavalrymen. The Union tide scattered the cavalrymen, smashing down the length of the Confederate entrenchments. They were soon joined by the 3rd Division of VI Corps, commanded by James Ricketts, on VI Corps' right flank. Lomax's cavalry was routed.

The only aggressive pursuit of the retreating Rebel army following Fisher's Hill was conducted by Devin's 2nd Brigade in the 1st Cavalry Division. Thomas Devin (center, with beard) and his brigade staff pose for a photographer at a manor house in the Shenandoah during the campaign. (AC)

Alerted by the sound of Crook's attack, the rest of VI Corps and XIX Corps joined in. Both corps stormed into the ravine separating the two armies, across Tumbling Run, and up the other side into the Confederate lines. Sheridan, on horseback, rushed along the Union lines shouting, "Forward! Forward everything! Go on, don't stop, go on!" Ramseur's Division crumbled, followed by Pegram's. Soon the rest of the Confederate line collapsed.

Shielded by Ramseur's and Pegram's divisions, Gordon's Division was able to fall back without disintegrating, but for John Gordon, the battle was over before it began. In his memoirs he summed up the entire battle in a single sentence: "to all experienced soldiers the story is told in one word—'flanked.'"

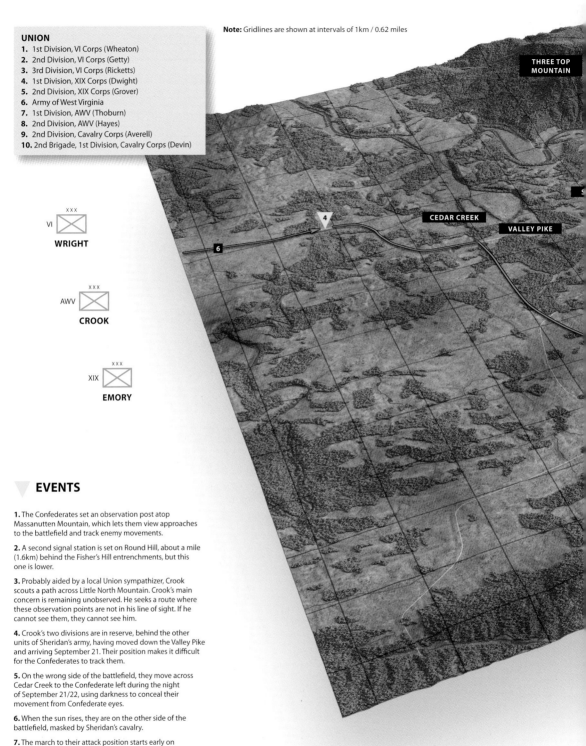

Note: Gridlines are shown at intervals of 1km / 0.62 miles

UNION
1. 1st Division, VI Corps (Wheaton)
2. 2nd Division, VI Corps (Getty)
3. 3rd Division, VI Corps (Ricketts)
4. 1st Division, XIX Corps (Dwight)
5. 2nd Division, XIX Corps (Grover)
6. Army of West Virginia
7. 1st Division, AWV (Thoburn)
8. 2nd Division, AWV (Hayes)
9. 2nd Division, Cavalry Corps (Averell)
10. 2nd Brigade, 1st Division, Cavalry Corps (Devin)

THREE TOP MOUNTAIN

CEDAR CREEK

VALLEY PIKE

VI — WRIGHT

AWV — CROOK

XIX — EMORY

▼ EVENTS

1. The Confederates set an observation post atop Massanutten Mountain, which lets them view approaches to the battlefield and track enemy movements.

2. A second signal station is set on Round Hill, about a mile (1.6km) behind the Fisher's Hill entrenchments, but this one is lower.

3. Probably aided by a local Union sympathizer, Crook scouts a path across Little North Mountain. Crook's main concern is remaining unobserved. He seeks a route where these observation points are not in his line of sight. If he cannot see them, they cannot see him.

4. Crook's two divisions are in reserve, behind the other units of Sheridan's army, having moved down the Valley Pike and arriving September 21. Their position makes it difficult for the Confederates to track them.

5. On the wrong side of the battlefield, they move across Cedar Creek to the Confederate left during the night of September 21/22, using darkness to conceal their movement from Confederate eyes.

6. When the sun rises, they are on the other side of the battlefield, masked by Sheridan's cavalry.

7. The march to their attack position starts early on September 22, requiring most of the day. The two divisions move through a series of ravines, shielded from Confederate observation. Additional precautions include having color bearers trail their flags, to prevent them from being spotted. Once they are across the mountain, they are hidden by woods.

8. To draw Confederate attention to their front and away from their left flank, Sheridan has VI Corps and XIX Corps demonstrate across from Pegram's and Gordon's divisions most of the morning and early afternoon.

9. Once in the woods, Crook forms up his two divisions for attack. He places them in line of battle, the two divisions alongside each other in parallel lines. The formations move silently down the mountainside, with orders to remain silent as they advance.

10. They encounter Confederate pickets, and drive them in. The two divisions of the Army of West Virginia move down on their enemy, shouting as they come.

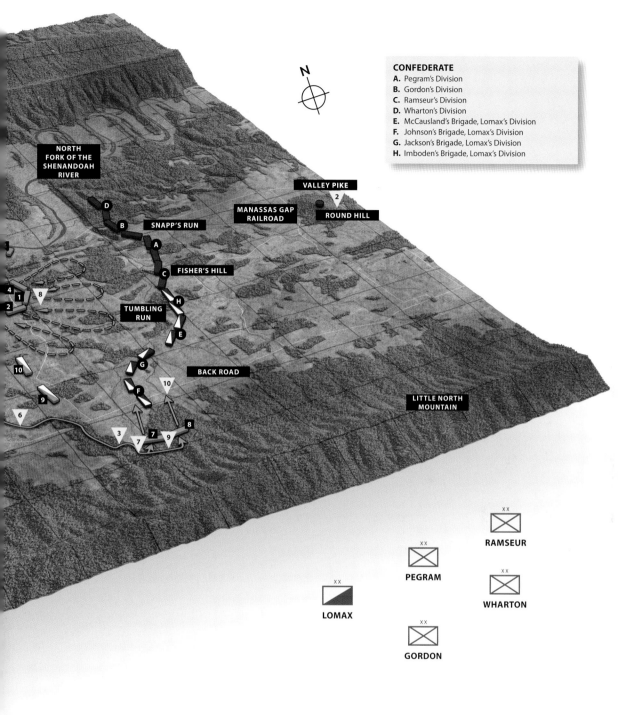

FLANKING THE CONFEDERATE ARMY AT FISHER'S HILL

The key to the Union victory at Fisher's Hill was Crook's flanking attack against the Confederate left. It hit the weakest portion of the Confederate line, held by an understrength dismounted cavalry division, allowing Crook's divisions to roll up Lomax's Division, and then in turn Ramseur's and Pegram's divisions. The maneuver seems likely to have originated from George Crook. He had fought in the Shenandoah previously and was familiar with the valley's terrain. He also had contacts in the valley. Both the knowledge and the contacts were put to good use.

While the bulk of Early's men were able to fall back from the battlefield, they had to abandon their artillery. The guns were at their revetments, ready to repel a Union assault, not limbered up for a retreat. The Union assault was so swift and from such an unexpected direction that these guns barely came into action before the Confederate lines were overwhelmed. Once the Union soldiers were in the lines, it was impossible to withdraw the artillery. Virtually all of Early's artillery remaining after Winchester, 14 guns, was captured.

In addition to the guns taken on the battlefield, Sheridan took over 1,100 prisoners and Early's army had an additional 30 killed and 210 wounded. The light mortality rate suffered by Early is a testimony to the level of surprise achieved by the Union army. The battle was over almost before the Confederates realized they were in a fight. Flight or surrender were the only options most of them were offered. In exchange, Sheridan's army suffered no more than 400 killed or wounded at Fisher's Hill.

The victory was not nearly as complete as Sheridan desired, however. Early's train, except wagons captured during pursuit, escaped. Early had readied his trains for departure during the night. The cavalry pursuit was not as vigorous as it should have been. Torbert, sent with Merritt's brigades to reinforce Wilson, had not pressed his attacks against Lee's Division on September 21. Instead, the next morning found him back at Front Royal, out of position to catch the retreating Confederates.

Of the cavalry still with Sheridan, only Devin's brigade from 1st Cavalry Division aggressively pursued Early. Despite a direct order from Sheridan to press Early, Averell's pursuit was slack. Devin's pursuit went unsupported. They snapped up stragglers. At a hill halfway between Fisher's Hill and Woodstock, they ran into a Confederate rearguard comprising two surviving Confederate field pieces and supporting infantry. Devin attacked. The defending troops scattered. The Confederate guns were captured, bringing the day's total bag to 16 guns captured. By then it was dark.

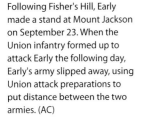

Following Fisher's Hill, Early made a stand at Mount Jackson on September 23. When the Union infantry formed up to attack Early the following day, Early's army slipped away, using Union attack preparations to put distance between the two armies. (AC)

The Union infantry spent most of the rest of September 22 at Fisher's Hill. Units were reformed, rearmed, and fed. Crook's command was left at Fisher's Hill to bury the dead and get some rest. VI and XIX corps continued down the Valley Pike, reaching Woodstock by the early morning of September 23. By mid-afternoon the two corps were in Edenburg, where they halted to await rations.

By then Early had slipped the trap. His troops moved through the gap at Narrow Passage where they could have been stopped, and were in Mount Jackson by morning. Devin's brigade caught up with Early's surviving main body on September 23, but it was too weak to dislodge the Confederates. They were forced to wait for reinforcements. It arrived in the form of Averell's cavalry division, which at 3.00pm launched a demonstration against Early.

Averell's attack was not pressed, however. Averell detected Confederate skirmishers on his right. Fearing being flanked and lacking infantry support, Averell withdrew. This allowed Early to break contact, and withdraw to Rude's Hill, halfway between New Market and Mount Jackson.

Sheridan was displeased by Averell's timidity. On September 24, he relieved Averell, giving command of the 2nd Division to Colonel William Powell, one of the division's brigade commanders. It was the beginning of a series of changes in the cavalry's command structure. When James Wilson was transferred to Tennessee, George Custer was promoted from one of the 1st Cavalry Division's brigadiers to divisional command of the 3rd Cavalry.

Regardless, Fisher's Hill, coming on the heels of the Third Battle of Winchester, gave Sheridan control of the Shenandoah Valley. Both armies had suffered roughly 5,000 casualties in the two fights, but the Army of the Valley was half the size of Sheridan's Army of the Shenandoah. Additionally, the Army of the Valley lost most of its guns. It could not win a stand-up battle against the Union forces until they were replaced.

THE BURNING, SEPTEMBER 24–OCTOBER 12

Early's retreat and Sheridan's pursuit continued for the next three days. On September 24 Early retreated from Rude's Hill through Harrisonburg, Virginia and from there headed down the Keezletown Road to Port Republic. He was dogged by Devin's brigade and the newly aggressive 2nd Cavalry Division. Several times the Union cavalry attempted to lure the Confederates into attacking by offering their flying batteries as bait, but Early was too canny to pause.

Early only turned to face his pursuers at sunset, forming a line of battle near Harrisburg and sending out skirmishers preparatory to bivouacking. The Union also bivouacked for the night, ready to battle at dawn. They woke to find Early gone. He had upped stakes and moved five miles further down the road after dark before setting up a fresh bivouac.

Morning saw Early's army marching towards Port Republic. Crossing the South Fork of the Shenandoah where it branches into the South River and Middle River, Early kept moving down the road to Browns Gap. He finally stopped his retreat in front of Browns Gap, covering the Shenandoah Valley approaches to this feature. Early's army had retreated 60 miles (100km).

On the morning of September 26, Early was finally in a position where he felt he could make a stand. He was joined by Kershaw's Division and Cutshaw's Battery, sent back by Robert E. Lee. His cavalry rejoined him there, as well. Lomax's Division had tried to cover the middle valley around Harrisonburg and Dayton, but had been driven out. Lee's Division had been forced down the Luray Valley. This division was joined by Rosser's Laurel Brigade, and Rosser assumed command of the division, which was thereafter called Rosser's Division.

Meanwhile, Sheridan had taken possession of most of the Shenandoah Valley. The VI and XIX corps pressed down the Valley Pike, reaching Harrisonburg on September 25. Torbert and his cavalry had stirred from Front Royal, pushed the Confederate cavalry out of Luray and its surrounding valley, crossed the South Fork of the Shenandoah, and crossed the Massanutten Mountain through the Massanutten Gap to reach New Market. The latter was already held by Union forces when Torbert arrived on the 25th.

Torbert's arrival gave Sheridan access to all his cavalry once again. Sheridan used them aggressively. On September 26 he sent Merritt, with a brigade from his 1st Cavalry Division, to reinforce Thomas Devin at Port Republic. Torbert, with the 3rd Cavalry Division and the Reserve Brigade from the 1st Cavalry, was sent on a long raid. They were to head down the Valley Pike to Staunton and from there move to Waynesboro, where they were to destroy the Virginia Central Railroad bridge where it crossed the South River.

Merritt reached Devin and helped him drive off the Confederate cavalry sent by Early to push the Yankees across the South River. Early then sent Kershaw's Division to clear Port Republic. Two brigades of cavalry could not hold against a complete and fresh infantry division. The Union cavalry fell back to Cross Keys, attempting to lure Kershaw to within reach of Sheridan's infantry. The attempt failed, largely because of Torbert's success.

Torbert struck Staunton with a fury. His troops destroyed arms, ammunition, tents, wagons, provisions, and fodder found there. Since Sheridan had no intention of moving south of Harrisonburg, he ordered Torbert to burn any mills and manufacturing buildings, and to drive off any livestock found. A swath of destruction followed Torbert's path along the Virginia Central Railroad. In addition to destroying buildings, the Union cavalry tore up the railroad tracks, and burned the wooden railroad bridge that crossed Christian's Creek. At Waynesboro they demolished the iron bridge across the South River, tossing the girders into the water. They failed only in their attempt to collapse the railroad tunnel at Rockfish Gap. Two Confederate artillery pieces covered by two companies of infantry beat the Union cavalry to the tunnel. Finding the tunnel protected, the cavalrymen decided to be satisfied with their accomplishments. Torbert had his men fall back.

It was as well. The raid alarmed Early, who swept down from Port Republic and Browns Gap to cover Waynesboro. Torbert was gone well before Early arrived. On September 29 Torbert camped at Bridgewater, southwest of Harrisonburg.

By then Sheridan had made a decision that shaped the rest of the campaign. Grant and Stanton were urging

Once Fisher's Hill had been taken, the upper valley was Sheridan's. The march of Sheridan's infantry up the valley was triumphant, albeit not as dramatic perhaps as depicted in this *Harpers Magazine* illustration. (AC)

Sheridan to push on to Staunton and Charlottesville—to occupy and hold the entire Shenandoah Valley—and then push on east of the Blue Ridge Mountains. It seemed so easy. Sheridan, at Harrisonburg, was deep in the valley, deeper than David Hunter had been earlier in 1864. Early's army was shattered and barely hanging on there.

Sheridan, on the scene, saw a different reality. The battles around Port Republic demonstrated that Early had stopped retreating, and was even willing to attack under the right circumstances. Even at Harrisonburg, Sheridan was at the end of a long and tenuous supply line. The Manassas Gap Railroad was unserviceable. The Winchester & Potomac was only just opening, and not yet a reliable supply route. His nearest railhead was at Martinsburg, 92 miles (148km) from Harrisonburg; from there, supplies had to move overland by wagon. Part of the reason Early escaped Union pursuit was because Sheridan had been forced to halt on two occasions to wait for rations.

Supply trains had to be convoyed by strong cavalry escorts. Two Confederate partisan ranger units were scouring the Union-held regions of the lower valley and territory around it. Even the Baltimore & Ohio Railroad was interdicted by partisans. The partisan cavalry was assisted by Confederate regular cavalry units in the middle valley, who were both scouting and raiding. These raiders forced massive escorts for supply trains. Even a regiment could be inadequate. Important trains were sometimes escorted by as many as 1,500 men.

Crossing the Blue Ridge Mountains to Charlottesville would nearly double the length wagon trains would travel. This would force Sheridan to use most of his cavalry to protect lines of communication. Even then, as long as the country around him was hostile to him and supporting the Confederates, Sheridan could not guarantee his army could be supplied. Without cavalry actively scouting Confederate-held territory, Sheridan's infantry would be in peril. It would only be a matter of time before an opponent as capable as Jubal Early ambushed an isolated corps or division, undoing the psychological impact of the Third Battle of Winchester and Fisher's Hill.

Moreover, Sheridan realized he need not hold the Shenandoah Valley. He merely had to deny its value to the Confederacy. Without the crops and livestock the valley produced, it was useless to the Confederacy. Fall was harvest season. It would take a year to replace what had been and was being harvested.

The inability of Early's army to stop Sheridan's led to increased reliance on guerrilla warfare by the Confederate partisan ranger units in the valley and in Loudoun County, east of the Blue Ridge Mountains on the Potomac River. Their efforts were successfully interdicting Union communications and supplies, but posed a threat only if Sheridan remained in the upper valley. (LOC)

Sheridan decided to withdraw to Winchester, destroying or seizing anything of value to the Confederacy in the regions he was abandoning. Doing this would shorten his supply lines while reducing the territory he needed to control. Any Confederate army attempting to retake the lower valley or raid into Maryland and Pennsylvania would be faced with the daunting task of transporting their own supplies overland from Staunton. It could not feed itself from locally available food and fodder, because when Sheridan was done, it would be

gone. The lower valley could be safely held with just Crook's forces. If things went as planned, troops borrowed from the Army of the Potomac could be returned.

Supply lines were not Sheridan's only concern. He was in hostile territory. Not even armed troops were immune from Confederate attack. The Confederates were quick to snap up isolated pockets of troops. In one instance, 150 Union cavalrymen picketing Mount Jackson were surprised by the 7th Virginia Cavalry and captured. They were sent back to Winchester under parole—a humiliation.

Few such incidents were as benign. Clashes between Confederate raiders and Union soldiers were frequent, especially at twilight or night when it was difficult to determine friend from foe until both parties were only a few yards apart. One such incident left Lieutenant John R. Meigs, Sheridan's engineer officer and a personal favorite, dead.

On October 3 Meigs and two other topographers were conducting a survey a few miles from Sheridan's headquarters. They were wearing dark raincoats. At dusk they encountered three other riders, dressed in blue. Thinking they were other Union soldiers, they rode up to the men. The other riders were Confederate cavalry scouts. Shots were exchanged. Meigs was killed, and another surveyor captured. The third escaped, and reported that Meigs had been shot by guerrillas while trying to surrender.

Initially the incident was treated by the North as illegal warfare by civilian irregulars. In reprisal, Sheridan ordered Dayton burned. Sheridan rescinded the order before it was carried out after the prisoner taken by the Confederates was released. He revealed Meigs had fired first, and was shot in response. Instead, Sheridan burned the buildings around the skirmish site, and took all able-bodied men in the area as prisoners of war.

Meigs's death occurred after Sheridan decided to withdraw back to Winchester. It was typical of conditions faced in the valley, however. Union soldiers resented this irregular warfare, and took out their resentment on anyone suspected of Confederate sympathies. This further alienated the civilian population, leading to more support for the Confederate raiders, and participation by civilians in partisan activities. This in turn provoked Union retribution, which prompted Confederate reprisals—a spiral of increasing violence by both sides.

Regardless, it was not until October 3 that Sheridan received Grant's assent to Sheridan's plans for withdrawal. Included were instructions that Sheridan was to, "Leave nothing for the subsistence of an army on any ground you abandon to the enemy." It was a directive Sheridan energetically followed.

Sheridan abandoned the upper valley rather than accept the risks inherent in maintaining an army at the end of a long, tenuous supply line. He opted to destroy anything of potential military value to the Confederacy. "The Burning," as residents later called it, left the valley covered in a pall of smoke from the torched barns, mills, and workshops. (LOC)

By October 2, Sheridan had replied, "All the crops, mills, etc., have been destroyed from Staunton to Mount Crawford ... I will make another raid with cavalry and infantry to Staunton and Lexington." It was only the beginning. On October 6 the Army of the Shenandoah departed Harrisonburg. The infantry corps marched down the Valley Pike to Winchester. The cavalry divisions spread the width of the Shenandoah Valley from the North Mountains to the Blue Ridge. They moved slowly north, destroying anything of military value to the Confederacy.

They burned barns, mills, haystacks, and any manufacturing buildings they found such as blacksmith shops or tanneries. Farmhouses were spared deliberate incineration, but some caught fire due to the proximity of nearby barns. Farmers who attempted force to save their property were killed. Pro-Union residents were occasionally spared, but others had their property burned along with Confederate-sympathizing neighbors. They were told they could apply to the Federal government for compensation after the war.

Nor could Early's army stop the devastation. Early's cavalry, led by Rosser, dogged the heels of the Yankee cavalry during Sheridan's withdrawal, but was unable to prevent the destruction. Finally, on October 8, an out of patience Sheridan ordered Torbert to deal with the Confederate cavalry. The following day, Torbert unleashed the 1st and 3rd Cavalry divisions against the Confederate horsemen. The Confederates were outnumbered nearly two to one. They were pushed back from Toms Brook, where the battle started, all the way to Woodstock, 20 miles (30km) away. The rout was so complete that the Union cavalrymen afterward called the battle "the Woodstock Races."

The Union army resumed its march north—and its pyrotechnics—following Toms Brook. On October 10 they reached Sheridan's destination: Cedar Creek. They camped north of the river.

In their wake they had left a cloud of smoke over the Shenandoah Valley. Between Harrisonburg and Woodstock alone over 2,000 barns and 70 mills had been burned. Over 4,000 cattle and 3,000 sheep had been driven ahead of the withdrawing Union soldiers. Between Staunton and Cedar Creek, 92 miles (148km) of valley from the Blue Ridge to the North Mountains was a ruined wasteland. The Shenandoah would not feed the Army of Northern Virginia that winter, nor could it feed the Army of the Valley. Its residents would be hard-put to feed themselves until the next harvest was brought in.

The burning of the valley—afterwards known by its inhabitants as "The Burning"—would be a source of resentment thereafter. Confederate citizens denounced Sheridan's action. Southern newspapers cried out for retribution. Sheridan's

By October 7, the Union army was north of Mount Jackson, its withdrawing infantry shielded by the Union cavalry. (AC)

THE CAPTURE OF THE CONFEDERATE CAVALRY'S BAGGAGE TRAIN AT TOMS BROOK (PP. 74–75)

Thomas Rosser and his brigade of cavalry were part of Fitzhugh Lee's Cavalry Division. They were known as the Laurel Brigade, from the custom of wearing a laurel sprig in their hats. Retained by Robert E. Lee when the rest of the division was originally sent to the Shenandoah Valley, it was finally sent there after the Confederate setbacks at the Third Battle of Winchester and Fisher's Hill.

From its arrival in the first week of October, Confederate loyalists held inflated expectations for both the commander and the brigade. They were hailed as "The Saviors of the Valley," even before entering combat. Rosser was given command of Fitzhugh Lee's Division, and made de facto commander of all cavalry in the valley.

Rosser attempted to live up to expectations, dogging the Union cavalry as they withdrew north. His cavalry failed to stop the Burning, but did succeed in irritating Sheridan. Finally, on October 8, Sheridan, fed up with the boldness of the Confederate cavalry, ordered Alfred Torbert to go after the Confederate cavalry the next morning, and "whip the Rebel cavalry or get whipped himself."

The next day Torbert sent his cavalry hunting. Custer's 3rd Division squared off against Rosser and Fitzhugh Lee's Division along the Back Road. Merritt's 1st Cavalry Division went after Lomax's Division down the Valley Pike.

The Confederate cavalry was badly outnumbered. Neither division had more than 2,000 men. Even with the reinforcements provided by the Laurel Brigade, the divisional totals present for battle were closer to 1,500 per division than 2,000 by this stage of the campaign. Rosser was far ahead of his own infantry, and could expect no support. Torbert's divisions were twice the size of their enemy's force, armed with repeating breechloaders (1), and well supplied.

The result was a Confederate rout. After an hour's struggle, the Confederate horse fled down the road. The Yankee cavalry chased them nearly 26 miles (40km). Custer's 3rd Division chased Rosser to Columbia Furnace; Merritt drove Lomax to Mount Jackson. The Rebel flight was so swift that the Yankees outstripped the Confederate artillery and baggage train (2). Rosser lost six cavalry guns and Lomax five, along with the caissons and teams pulling them. The Union cavalry (3) also captured ambulances, a battery forge, and 47 baggage wagons—almost everything on wheels. These included the headquarters wagons of Rosser, Lomax, Wickham, and Pollard (4), along with the generals' personal baggage.

The Union army would later call the battle "The Woodstock Races," due to the speed at which it was fought. The defeat dispirited the Confederate cavalry, and sealed Union mounted superiority in the valley. While the Confederate cavalry would prove effective as partisans, and support the Army of the Valley in its future battles, it would never again independently challenge the Union's cavalry in the field.

actions puzzled the Army of the Valley's leadership. Early considered them the actions of a coward. Gordon did not understand why Sheridan had not sought a final battle with the Confederate army. They were demoralized, outnumbered, and starving. The Union army was well supplied, and flushed with victory.

Neither man realized what Sheridan had done. Burning the Shenandoah Valley achieved Sheridan's strategic goals without the necessity for a battle and the casualties a battle entailed. Withdrawal reduced Mosby's and McNeill's raids from a peril to a nuisance. Sheridan valued the lives of his men more than he valued the property or convenience of the valley's inhabitants. The Burning was hard on the Shenandoah Valley's civilians but, as Sheridan saw it, these were the people that were sheltering the men bushwhacking his soldiers. If they preferred Union occupation to devastation, they should have submitted to occupation quietly.

Thomas Rosser was George Custer's West Point roommate and friend. On October 9 Custer commanded the 3rd Cavalry Division of Sheridan's army, while Rosser commanded the Confederate cavalry. At the beginning of the Battle of Toms Brook, Custer saw Rosser, and saluted him. (LOC)

As far as Sheridan was concerned, the Shenandoah Valley Campaign was over. He had done everything asked of him, except capturing the Virginia Central Railroad. Even that had been badly damaged by his men. The valley was no longer a source of supply for Robert E. Lee's army, and was useless as a highway along which to invade the North. All that there remained to do was picket the lower valley and return the borrowed troops to Grant.

Jubal Early might not have agreed with Sheridan's assessment. To dispute it, Early would have to bring a defeated army with dispirited cavalry across a swath of devastation. He planned exactly that.

CEDAR CREEK, OCTOBER 13–20

United States Marine Corps General James Mattis once said, "No war is over until the enemy says it's over. We may think it over, we may declare it over, but in fact, the enemy gets a vote." Both the Union and the Confederacy illustrated the truth of that aphorism at the Battle of Cedar Creek. The Union assumed the campaign in the Shenandoah Valley was over when Early did not, and the Confederates assumed the battle was over when Sheridan did not.

Once Rosser's Brigade arrived on October 5, Early planned to counterattack Sheridan's army. In his memoirs, Early states he began planning an attack at Harrisonburg that day only to discover the Union infantry abandoning the position on the following day. Early followed Sheridan back down the valley. Lomax's horse reoccupied the Luray Valley and Rosser's Division (formerly Fitzhugh Lee's Division) pursued the Union rearguard up the Valley Pike. Except for cavalry skirmishing and the cavalry battle at Toms Brook, the two sides did not engage.

Once camped at Cedar Creek, Sheridan began planning a drawdown of his army. After ordering the withdrawal, Sheridan informed Grant that all of the borrowed troops could be removed, leaving control of the lower valley to Crook's Army of West Virginia. Grant decided to recall only VII Corps and one of the two cavalry divisions originally with the Army of the Potomac. These units were ordered withdrawn on October 11, and sent to Front Royal.

Washington had not given up on taking Charlottesville, however. On October 12 General Henry Halleck, Grant's chief of staff, sent Sheridan a telegram requesting operations against Gordonsville and Charlottesville. Taking these towns would reduce Richmond's railroad access to the rest of the Confederacy to just one railroad. The following day Sheridan received a second telegram, this one from Secretary of War Edwin Stanton, requesting a conference in Washington to discuss operations. Headquarters knew Sheridan was reluctant to mount an expedition to Charlottesville. Stanton wanted an opportunity to personally impress Sheridan with its necessity. Prior to receiving the second telegram Sheridan sent orders for Wright's VI Corps to wait at Front Royal, and ordered Torbert's Cavalry Corps to join them.

On October 13, three days after the Army of the Shenandoah encamped north of Cedar Creek, Early's Army of the Valley returned to their old positions at Fisher's Hill. The Union army used Hupp's Hill as a springboard during the Battle of Fisher's Hill. Early sent Conner's Brigade from Kershaw's Division to occupy Hupp's Hill. Crook's forces countered. Crook sent his 1st Division, commanded by Colonel Joseph Thoburn, to drive off the Confederates.

An artillery duel opened the action. Union infantry from two brigades of the 1st Division attacked, seeking to capture the Confederate guns. The brigades became separated during the attack, and Conner's Brigade flanked the 1st Brigade of 1st Division. The 1st Brigade was pushed back with heavy casualties. Its commander George Wells was mortally wounded and captured. As the Confederate occupation was intended as a reconnaissance in force, Conner's Brigade withdrew to Fisher's Hill. The Union suffered 214 casualties, and the Confederates over 180, including Brigadier-General James Conner, who lost a leg.

Until Hupp's Hill the Union assumed that Early's infantry had fallen back to Charlottesville. This action revealed the Army of the Valley close at hand. Sheridan ordered VI Corps back. It rejoined the Army of the Shenandoah, arriving at noon on October 14.

At first Sheridan saw Early's move as an opportunity for a cavalry raid on Charlottesville, to destroy the Virginia Central. He took the cavalry with him to Front Royal on October 15, but sent it back the next day. Horatio Wright, commander of VI Corps and acting commander of the army in Sheridan's absence, reported Confederate reinforcements. Sheridan pressed on to his meeting in Washington.

Initial Confederate scouting showed the Union army was too well dug in for a direct assault, but Early was determined to attack. He believed that if he could beat the Yankees one more time—as he had so often done before—he could regain control of the Shenandoah Valley.

The Confederate army caught the Union one literally sleeping. The first indication many members of Crook's corps and XIX Corps got that they were under attack were the bayonets of Confederate infantrymen in their tents. (AC)

The plan of attack came from a suggestion by Major-General John Gordon. Early knew a successful attack required flanking the Union lines on the Union right. Towards that end, on October 16 he sent Rosser's cavalry to probe the enemy's position. To cover Rosser's withdrawal, he brought the rest of his army forward, a demonstration that fixed Union attention to their right.

Dissatisfied with Early's initial plan, Gordon had gone to a Confederate observation post atop Massanutten Mountain. From the post the entire area could be viewed. Gordon saw the Union army positioned for an attack against their right flank, but unprepared for a blow to their left flank. The latter was protected by the impassable Massanutten Mountain.

Were the mountains really impassable? Gordon thought he saw a path through the mountain. He personally examined it. He found a dim and narrow pathway, so narrow that at points it could be crossed only one man at a time. Gordon drew up a new plan. His own, Ramseur's, and Pegram's divisions would fall on the Union army's unprotected left, while the rest of Early's army pinned down the Union right. When Early saw this proposal, he adopted it, withdrawing his army to Fisher's Hill to prepare for the attack.

The Union army spent two quiet days while Early prepared his assault. The various probes, demonstrations, and attacks on the Union right convinced the Yankees that any attack from Early would come from the right. The three infantry corps had encamped in a north–south line, with Crook's corps on a hill one mile north of the North Fork of the Shenandoah River. XIX Corps was on the next hill north of Crook's encampment, and VI Corps was on a hill just north of that one. All three had their western flank protected by Cedar Creek. To strengthen the natural rampart provided by the creek, all three corps threw up entrenchments behind Cedar Creek. The south flank was covered by the seemingly impassable Massanutten Mountain. The Union cavalry was encamped north of VI Corps, just west of Middletown.

The common soldiers in Sheridan's army had convinced themselves the Confederates would not attack. Plans to return VI Corps to Grant fed a feeling the campaign was over. The officers knew that Early had no way to feed his troops from the devastated valley and lacked the wagons to move enough food 75 miles (120km) along the Valley Pike from Staunton. He either had to attack or retreat in the next few days. He could not successfully attack across Cedar Creek, so he was bound to head home. Vigilance slacked, and pickets relaxed.

Sheridan, however, was unable to relax. He met with Stanton at the War Department on the morning of October 17. He left Washington at noon, taking a train to Martinsburg, West Virginia. He left Martinsburg the next morning, riding to Winchester escorted by a regiment of cavalry. He arrived at 4.00pm, and surveyed the heights around Winchester to place fortifications. He received a report that everything was quiet at Cedar Creek, and decided to spend the

By 9.00am the Confederate army had achieved its objective: the capture of Sheridan's headquarters, Belle Grove House. The Confederate soldiers went through the encampments of three Union infantry corps to reach it. (LOC)

night in Winchester. At 6.00am he awoke, receiving a report that artillery fire was being heard at Cedar Creek. Early was beginning his attack.

The Confederate army had spent the night of October 18/19 sneaking over the Massanutten Mountain. They were in position by 4.30am, lined up on the unprotected south flank of Crook's corps-sized Army of West Virginia. Three divisions—Gordon's and Ramseur's leading, with Pegram's Division close behind—smashed into Crook's encampment behind the fortifications intended to protect them. Kershaw's Division struck across the minimally manned fortifications.

Crook's three divisions were scattered in less than an hour. Most of the troops were in their tents, asleep when the Confederate wave struck. Fog made it impossible to see. Most of those awake assumed the Confederate assault was coming from the west, where the 1st Division was camped, and where Kershaw's men were attacking. As it was, Kershaw successfully captured the works guarding the 1st Division, including the artillery there, in the opening minutes of his attack. He took the captured guns and turned them on their previous owners. As the unready men of 1st Division were forming to counterattack, they were hit in the flank by Gordon's Division.

The 2nd Division, commanded that day by (future US President) Colonel Rutherford B. Hayes, fared no better. Nor did the one-brigade Provisional Division. Both were struck from an unexpected direction by Ramseur's Division as orders were given to assist the 1st Division.

Everywhere men were faced with the choice of flight, death, or surrender. Most fled into the fog, which shielded their retreat. Those who attempted to fight, including the 1st Division's commander, Colonel Joseph Thoburn, were killed. A total of 530 men in Crook's corps surrendered, many caught in their bedrolls. In addition, the ambulance train, supply wagons, and camp equipment were lost.

Crook's corps temporarily ceased existence, leaving XIX Corps uncovered. The latter was a little better prepared than Crook's command. The 2nd Division and one brigade of the 1st Division had been roused just before the Confederate attack began. They had woken early to prepare for a reconnaissance in force scheduled later that morning. Musketry from the direction of Crook's encampment gave a few minutes warning, but the fog hid the Confederate approach and confusion reigned about its direction. The awakened troops formed to meet the enemy.

The Union gunners fought for their pieces at Cedar Creek, but the enemy advance proved too swift to allow the artillerymen to withdraw their cannon. Most were recaptured at the battle's end. (LOC)

Everyone assumed the attack was coming from the west and the corps deployed accordingly. They prepared to meet the attacks from Wharton's Division, beginning its attack, and Kershaw's men, finishing up Crook's 1st Division. Suddenly, they were hit from the flank and rear by the three divisions Gordon was commanding. XIX Corps collapsed as quickly as Crook's divisions had. The 114th New York suffered 185 casualties in a few minutes, nearly half its roster, fighting to hold the rear. XIX Corps suffered most of the day's 1,500 casualties in this initial assault, including over 200 men taken

The Battle of Cedar Creek—the morning.

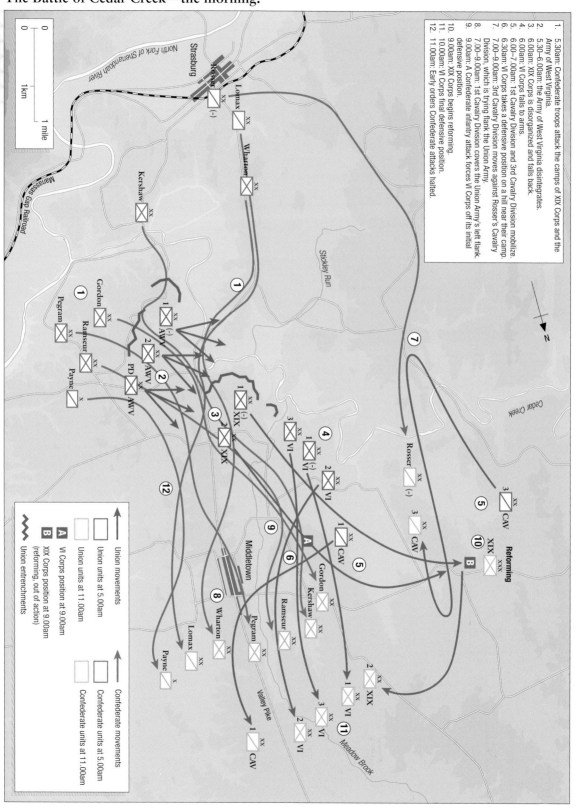

1. 5.30am: Confederate troops attack the camps of XIX Corps and the Army of West Virginia.
2. 5.30–6.00am: the Army of West Virginia disintegrates.
3. 6.00am: XIX Corps is disorganized and falls back.
4. 6.00am: VI Corps falls to arms.
5. 6.00–7.00am: 1st Cavalry Division mobilize.
6. 6.30am: VI Corps takes a defensive position on a hill near their camp.
7. 7.00–9.00am: 3rd Cavalry Division moves against Rosser's Cavalry Division, which is trying flank the Union Army.
8. 7.00–9.00am: 1st Cavalry Division covers the Union Army's left flank.
9. 9.00am: A Confederate infantry attack forces VI Corps off its initial defensive position.
10. 9.00am: XIX Corps begins reforming.
11. 10.00am: VI Corps final defensive position.
12. 11.00am: Early orders Confederate attacks halted.

THREE TOP MOUNTAIN

NORTH FORK OF THE SHENANDOAH RIVER

CONFEDERATE
A. Gordon's Corps (the initial position of the units that flanked the Union)
B. Pegram's Division
C. Gordon's Division
D. Ramseur's Division
E. Wharton's Division
F. Kershaw's Division
G. Payne's Brigade, Rosser's Division

GORDON

STRASBURG

TUMBLING RUN

FISHER'S HILL

EVENTS

1. Preparations begin at the Confederate camp. Men are briefed on the plan. The need for silence and speed is emphasized. Troops are stripped of canteens and anything that might clatter or make noise. Sword belts, if taken, are muffled.

2. The assault force leaves camp at 8.00pm on October 18, once night has fallen, and full dark has arrived.

3. Men snake through the scouted pathway, silently, guided by the couriers along the way. The moon rises just before 10.00pm. For the rest of the night, their path is lit by a waning three-quarter moon.

4. Once past Massanutten Mountain, the 9,000 men of Gordon's, Ramseur's, and Pegram's divisions form into their units.

5. They then ford the North Fork of the Shenandoah River, frigid in the chilly October night.

6. Now on the same side of Cedar Creek as the three Union infantry corps, they move along a wagon road until they are in their assault positions, less than 500 yards from the Army of West Virginia's camp. By 4.30am the Confederates are in position. The Yankees are asleep, unaware of the threat.

7. Early's remaining infantry—Kershaw's and Wharton's divisions—along with all of the army's artillery are moving down the Valley Pike into Strasburg. The two divisions separate.

8. Wharton and the artillery continue down the Pike.

9. Kershaw's Division takes a road running east from Strasburg, and then to a ford across Cedar Creek.

10. The Confederates' ultimate goal is Sheridan's headquarters, Belle Grove House, to the west of the Valley Pike and the rear of XIX Corps. To reach it, they would have to go through both Crook's Corps and XIX Corps.

11. Shortly after the Confederates reach their position, a thick morning fog rolls in. Visibility drops to a yard. The fog muffles sound and distorts its direction. At 5.30am, before reveille sounds, the Confederates attack, rushing into the sleeping Union camps with the Rebel yell.

CROSSING MASSANUTTEN MOUNTAIN

Major-General John Gordon found a trail across Massanutten Mountain permitting access to the Union left flank. The path was narrow. There were places men had to pass single file, and neither mounted horses nor artillery could manage the trail. It would require surprise and timing to achieve success. Before the attack Gordon placed guides at each fork and crossway on the route, to direct traffic and to ensure the files went the right direction. At one point on the route, scouts thought they saw two enemy pickets, only to discover the shadows were two cedar bushes. At another point, a felled tree marking the route was discovered to have been moved by a local farmer, unaware of its significance. The correct path was again marked.

LOOTING THE UNION CAMP AT CEDAR CREEK (PP. 84–85)

By 9.00am the Army of the Valley had captured the camps of all three Union corps. The camps contained the tent, bedding, and soldiers' personal equipment abandoned in hurried flight. Haversacks, canteens, knapsacks, greatcoats, and shoes had been left behind. In addition, corps trains, filled with food, medicine, spare clothing, blankets, and tents had been abandoned.

Luxuries such as coffee, chocolate, and canned food lay scattered around the camp. So did waterproof raincoats and tarps, good marching boots, cooking pots, frying pans, and other camp gear. Some pots contained food, which was being prepared for post-reveille breakfast.

Early's soldiers had been on short commons even before returning to Fisher's Hill. They spent nearly a week at Fisher's Hill short of everything except determination. There was no food in the valley south of Fisher's Hill. The Confederate commissariat had too few wagons to move sufficient rations from Staunton to feed Early's army. They were hungry even before beginning their march over Massenutten Mountain, and most had not eaten breakfast that morning. If they had, it was cold meat and hard tack stored in a pocket. Many were barefoot (1), and possessed inadequate clothing to protect them against the seasonal cold. Their weapons were worn out.

The temptation proved irresistible for some soldiers in Early's army. It was an opportunity for a hot meal, a chance at a cup of coffee, virtually unknown in the South for at least a year. The Confederate divisions disintegrated as thoroughly as the Union

infantry had earlier. Men ate the food prepared for their enemies (2). They filled their stomachs, perhaps the first time they had stuffed themselves in a week. Then they filled haversacks with coffee, sugar, and biscuits or tinned food. Then they discarded their worn haversacks for new, Yankee issue.

While they were at it, many sought out a fresh pair of boots (3), some new shirts, and trousers (4) to replace ones the bottoms were falling out of. Winter was coming. Getting a warm greatcoat—even if it was Union issue—was an opportunity worth seizing. Some wool blankets were worth grabbing, too, especially since the Confederate quartermaster was unlikely to supply them later on. When else would a soldier get an opportunity to replace a worn-out rifle with one of the brand-new Springfields (5) lying around abandoned?

The common soldiers believed they had licked the Yankees— that the Yankees would run, and keep on running. They had been marching all night and fighting all morning. They wanted a reward. Their officers sensed the mood of their men. They knew the first rule of giving orders: never give an order that will not be obeyed. So they watched as their men looted the Union encampments. Given a few hours, they would be ready to fight again.

It might have made a difference if Jubal Early had been ready to keep pushing. He was convinced the battle was won. So the Confederate advance paused, giving the Union army precious time to reorganize.

prisoner. Additionally, it lost 11 cannon, when Gordon's advance prevented their withdrawal.

It was now the turn of VI Corps. Encamped the furthest north of the three infantry corps, it had been 1.5 miles (2km) from where the Confederates launched their attack. That distance, and the time it took for the Rebel troops to fight through Crook's corps and XIX Corps, gave VI Corps time to turn out. Additionally, the morning fog was dissipating, and visibility restored. Regardless, it too was pushed back. It retreated in good order

to a knoll east of its encampment, southwest of the town of Middleton. Once there, VI Corps was attacked by four Confederate divisions—Gordon's, Wharton's, Ramseur's, and Pegram's. VI Corps retreated to the next ridgeline, but it did not break.

It was 9.00am. VI Corps was the last organized infantry on the battlefield. The Union cavalry had already responded to the attack. Custer's 3rd Cavalry Division was engaging Rosser's cavalry on the west flank. Rosser was tasked with severing the Valley Pike, to cut off any retreat by the fleeing Union infantry. Custer's men had prevented this, but they had their hands full, and could not directly aid VI Corps. Wesley Merritt's 1st Cavalry Division was covering VI Corps' left, but it was insufficient to stop a concerted push by the rest of the Confederate cavalry supported by infantry. XIX Corps was reforming, but only its 2nd Division was in a condition to aid VI Corps. Crook's infantry was streaming north. One final strong Confederate push at 9.00am—as General Gordon was then urging Early to make—would have sealed the victory.

It never came. VI Corps was withdrawing—to a new defensive line, not off the battlefield. The Confederates did not realize that. Early decided a final attack was unnecessary. Many of the common soldiers decided the battle was over, and began looting the camps of Crook's corps and XIX Corps. A lull developed, which gave the Union army an opportunity to reform. Against all Confederate expectations, except perhaps those of John Gordon, the Union army was doing just that.

Sheridan had been roused from sleep at 6.00am with a report of a battle at Cedar Creek. Initially he believed the fighting was XIX Corps' reconnaissance in force. By the time he left Winchester, between 8.00 and 9.00am, he was aware it was a major battle. Only as he rode south did he realize its magnitude. When he saw the numbers of stragglers heading for the rear, he understood how badly the morning was going.

At first he considered withdrawing the army to Winchester, forming a new line, and confronting Early there. Instead he decided to fight it out at Cedar Creek. He felt his men still believed in him. All he had to do was rally them. He began what became known as "Sheridan's Ride."

Sheridan was absent, in Winchester, when the battle started. Despite the magnitude of the initial Confederate success, Sheridan chose to fight at Cedar Creek. He rode 14 miles (22km) to the battlefield, successfully rallying his men in what became known as "Sheridan's Ride." (LOC).

Following a disastrous morning, the Army of the Shenandoah had been steadied, rallied, and reorganized for attack during the afternoon. At 4.00pm Sheridan launched his counterattack, which swept the Confederate army off the field of battle. (AC)

Mounted on his black horse Rienzi, accompanied by two aides, he rode down the Valley Pike, waving his hat to groups of demoralized soldiers. As he passed he told them, "If I had been with you this morning this disaster would not have happened. We must face the other way; we will go back and recover our camp."

It worked. His men followed him, heartened by Sheridan's presence and confidence. Word spread to those that had not seen their chief. They turned around, too, heading towards battle again. He rode 14 miles (22km), through Newtown, before finding his army, comprising two VI Corps divisions. XIX Corps was at his right and rear, reforming. A third VI Corps division, Getty's 2nd Division, was ahead. Sheridan left orders to halt and reform. Then he rode to the front.

There he found the 2nd Division and Torbert's cavalry a mile north of Middletown. They were the only Union forces still in contact with the enemy. He told them to hold fast. Behind Getty's 2nd Division he found the remnants of Crook's corps—regimental color guards that had reformed in the rear, led by Rutherford Hayes. Sheridan began to plan an attack.

At 1.00pm Early's army made an attack, but it was repulsed. The Confederate attack fizzled. This gave Sheridan time to reorganize and reform his army. By 4.00pm he was ready. He had 25,000 infantry: VI Corps on the left, XIX on the right, and Crook's Corps reforming in the rear. Merritt's division covered the Union left flank, and Custer's the right. Early's army was ready for them, formed in five divisions of infantry, its artillery augmented by captured Union guns. They were outnumbered two to one. They had marched all night and fought all day. They were in the open. Sheridan's army advanced and swept away the Confederate line.

Major-General Stephen Ramseur commanded the Confederate rearguard during the afternoon retreat. He was shot and mortally wounded attempting to rally his men. (AC)

The Confederate resistance was tenacious, but the Union charge was too strong. Early's men began to fall back, slowly at first, then faster. Finally they routed, rushing back to their positions at Fisher's Hill. The planking on the bridge across the Shenandoah below Strasburg collapsed. The Union artillery, wagons, and ambulances taken that morning were trapped on the Union side of the river. So was most of the Confederate artillery. All of their morning's spoils were lost, along with their own guns.

Union cavalry began a relentless pursuit of the fleeing Rebels. Some 1,200 prisoners were taken. Among them was a mortally wounded Major-General Stephen Ramseur, shot while rallying his men. Only darkness halted the pursuit, and prevented the capture of the rest of Early's army.

The Battle of Cedar Creek—the afternoon.

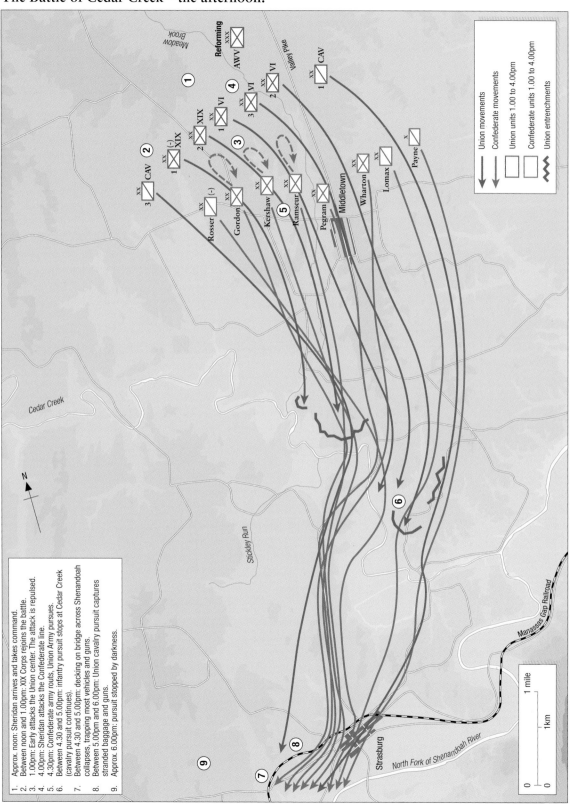

1. Approx. noon: Sheridan arrives and takes command.
2. Between noon and 1.00pm: XIX Corps rejoins the battle.
3. 1.00pm: Early attacks the Union center. The attack is repulsed.
4. 4.00pm: Sheridan attacks the Confederate line.
5. 4.30pm: Confederate army routs, Union Army pursues.
6. Between 4.30 and 5.00pm: infantry pursuit stops at Cedar Creek (cavalry pursuit continues).
7. Between 4.30 and 5.00pm: decking on bridge across Shenandoah collapses, trapping most vehicles and guns.
8. Between 5.00pm and 6.00pm: Union cavalry pursuit captures stranded baggage and guns.
9. Approx. 6.00pm: pursuit stopped by darkness.

Union movements
Confederate movements
Union units 1.00 to 4.00pm
Confederate units 1.00 to 4.00pm
Union entrenchments

89

AFTERMATH

Sheridan's Shenandoah Valley Campaign effectively ended with the victory at Cedar Creek. The victory helped ensure Lincoln's re-election in November. Early's shattered army withdrew to Staunton. From there, Lee transferred most of the remaining units back to Petersburg. Lee left Early in the Shenandoah, a commander without an army. The decision was half politics and half punishment. Relieving Early would signal the magnitude of the Cedar Creek disaster, and hurt Confederate morale. Leaving Early to rusticate in the valley also signaled Lee's displeasure.

Thomas Rosser became one of three Civil War Confederate generals to serve as general officers in the United States Army during the Spanish–American War of 1898. (LOC)

VI Corps, one division of XIX Corps, and one division of the Army of West Virginia joined the Army of the Potomac in November. Crook and the Kanawha Division returned to West Virginia. Sheridan was left with one infantry division from XIX Corps and the Cavalry Corps. Both armies went into winter quarters in November, Sheridan at Winchester, Early at Staunton.

The fighting in the valley would go on for another six months, with Mosby's Rangers more active than ever. In February 1865 they even captured Brigadier-General George Crook. Their efforts were never more than a nuisance, however. They lacked the strength to drive the hated Yankees out of the lower Shenandoah.

While they picked off a few isolated garrisons and working parties, Mosby's efforts hurt the valley's inhabitants more than the enemy. Hunger stalked the Shenandoah Valley that winter. Sheridan fought Washington for food relief, and finally won. Emergency rations for civilians were shipped to Winchester in late winter. Yet Mosby's raiders made moving food into the valley more difficult, slowing the flow of supplies that fed everyone, including the suffering civilians.

In February 1865 Sheridan finally moved. In March he defeated Early's skeletal army at Waynesboro, and took Charlottesville. From there he rejoined Grant, taking an active part in the closing stages of the Appomattox Campaign.

After the war, the Union leaders in Sheridan's army prospered professionally. Sheridan rose to command the United States Army. Rutherford Hayes and William McKinley became US Presidents. Crook, Wilson, and Custer played important roles in the Indian Wars of the 1870s and 1880s.

Three of the leaders in the campaign—Wesley Merritt, Thomas Rosser, and Fitzhugh Lee—would fight a second war together. This time they fought on the same side, as generals in the United States Army during the Spanish–American War.

Early spent the rest of his life defending his professional reputation, and creating the "Lost Cause" movement, arguing the Union won through overwhelming force rather than martial prowess. It was less painful than admitting he had been outgeneraled by Sheridan as other Confederate generals had by Grant and Sherman. The harshest critics of Jubal Early were his subordinate generals, however.

The Shenandoah Campaign, especially the victory at Cedar Creek, was a refutation of claims that the Union lacked military skill or leadership. Sheridan fought brilliantly at both the strategic and tactical levels. Harsh as "The Burning" was, it achieved Sheridan's strategic goals. He refused to cede to Confederate expectations, presenting them with an option they could not counter.

Similarly, his performance at Cedar Creek, rallying a shattered army and then leading them to a crushing victory, demonstrated superior leadership. His presence, and only his presence, yielded victory. He could be harsh. He made occasional mistakes, but in the end he always won.

XIX Corps parading in the Grand Review following the end of the Civil War. (AC)

THE BATTLEFIELD TODAY

The Shenandoah Valley is large, and the sites where the battles were fought are numerous and scattered. Despite recent efforts at battlefield preservation, some of the battlefields have been lost forever. Most of the Guard Hill battlefield is the site of an interstate highway intersection, permanently altered by highway construction.

Another threat to the battlefields is Interstate Highway 81. It parallels the old Valley Pike, and bisects the Winchester, Cedar Creek, Fisher's Hill, and Toms Brook battlefields. Proposed upgrades to the interstate include widening it to six lanes throughout the valley, with eight- to twelve-lane expansion in urban areas. This will alter a significant portion of the battlefields over which it passes.

Yet parts of the important battlefields have been preserved. In 2002 the Cedar Creek and Belle Grove National Historical Park was established, preserving both part of the Cedar Creek battlefield and the Belle Grove Plantation, which served as Sheridan's headquarters during the battle. About half of the area of the park is privately owned, but the park offers driving tours, both self-directed and ranger-led, along the public roads that cross the battlefield.

The Belle Grove House was Sheridan's headquarters during the Battle of Cedar Creek. The house has been preserved, and is part of the Cedar Creek and Belle Grove National Historic Park. (LOC)

The non-profit Cedar Creek Battlefield Foundation runs the Hupp's Hill Civil War Park at that site, and sponsors an annual re-enactment of the Battle of Cedar Creek on the weekend closest to the battle. Their website (www.cedarcreekbattlefield.org) has more information about their activities and battlefield preservation efforts.

Portions of the Fisher's Hill and Toms Brook battlefields can also be viewed. Maps for self-directed tours of the Fisher's Hill battlefields can be obtained in Strasburg and other local communities, and there are several wayside markers on the battlefield, which can be reached on public roads. The Valley Pike and Fisher's Hill Trail Project is creating a trail system through the battlefield that connects with Strasburg.

A section of the Toms Brook battlefield is part of Shenandoah County Park. This includes a historical marker. Another part of the battlefield is now a golf course and driving range.

The various Winchester battlefields have been altered by urban expansion at Winchester, Virginia, but about 600 acres of the "Third" battlefield have been preserved north of the Berryville Pike around Redbud Run. The area offers hiking trails and a self-guided tour of the site of some of the fiercest fighting to take place during the battle.

Sheridan's campaign was not the only set of battles fought in the Shenandoah Valley. The battles described in this book are a subset of the combat in the Shenandoah. Other battlefields are preserved in the Shenandoah Valley. In many ways, both Jackson's 1862 Valley Campaign and the battles fought in the spring and early summer of 1864 receive more attention from the local population than the battles of Sheridan's Shenandoah campaign. This makes sense. The home team *won* those matches, after all.

If you are interested in visiting the various Shenandoah Valley battlefields and Civil War museums, the Shenandoah Valley Battlefields Foundation website (www.shenandoahatwar.org) is a good starting point for planning your trip.

The bronze equestrian statue honoring Phil Sheridan in Sheridan Circle, Washington DC. The statue depicts Sheridan waving his hat, as if rallying his men. (LOC)

FURTHER READING

Much has been written about the Civil War in the Shenandoah. As with battlefield preservation, more attention has been given to Jackson's 1862 campaigns than the 1864 campaigns, especially Sheridan's campaign. There is a lot available, despite this.

The place for a historian to start is in the pertinent volumes of *The War of the Rebellion: A Compilation of the Official Records of the Union and Confederate Armies*. Published by the War Department after the Civil War, it is a massive documentary collection drawn from the official dispatches of both sides. It is available online at Cornell's *Making of America* website (http://moa.library.cornell.edu).

For those seeking more readable presentations, I recommend memoirs of the participating generals, especially those written by Sheridan, Early, Gordon, and Crook. Care must be exercised, as all four, especially Early, seek to put their actions in the best light. Another source worth reading is the fourth volume of *Battles and Leaders of the Civil War*. This was a collection of accounts written by participants. Originally published in *Century Magazine*, the articles were republished in book form in the 1880s. It is still in print.

All of these books, as well as many of the other 19th- and early 20th-century sources the author has used, are now available online at Google Books (http://books.google.com), the Internet Archives (http://archive.org), and Project Gutenberg (http://www.gutenberg.org). These resources make the American Civil War one of the most accessible conflicts to modern readers.

Sheridan and his generals pose for photographs in Winchester after a victorious campaign. The officers differ from the photo taken in his last days as commander of the Cavalry Corps. From left to right, those pictured are Wesley Merritt, Philip Sheridan, George Crook, James Forsyth (Sheridan's chief of staff), and George Custer. (LOC)

Crowninshield, Benjamin William, *The Battle of Cedar Creek, October 19, 1864: A Paper Read Before the Military Historical Society of Massachusetts, December 8, 1879*, Riverside Press, Cambridge, Massachusetts, 1879

Dyer, Frederick H., *A Compendium of the War of the Rebellion* (3 vols), The Dyer Publishing Co., Des Moines, Iowa, 1908

Early, Jubal Anderson, *A Memoir of the Last Year of the War for Independence in the Confederate States of America*, Charles W. Button, Lynchburg, Virginia, 1867

Gordon, John Brown, *Reminiscences of the Civil War*, Charles Scribner's Sons, New York, 1904

Grant, Ulysses S., *Personal Memoirs of U.S. Grant*, Charles Webster, New York, 1885

Hearn, Chester G., *Six Years of Hell: Harpers Ferry During the Civil War*, Louisiana State University Press, Baton Rouge, Louisiana 1999

Johnson, Robert Underwood and Buel, Clarence Clough, *Battles and Leaders of the Civil War*, vol. 4, The Century Company, New York 1887

Pond, George Edward, *The Shenandoah Valley in 1864*, Charles Scribner's Sons, New York, 1912

Sheridan, Philip H., *Personal Memoirs of P.H. Sheridan*, Charles L. Webster and Co., New York, 1888

Sifakis, Stewart, *Compendium of the Confederate Armies: Virginia*, Facts on File, New York, 1992

US War Department, *The War of the Rebellion: A Compilation of the Official Records of the Union and Confederate Armies*, series 1, vol. 43. Washington, DC, GPO, 1893

Walker, Aldace F., *The Vermont Brigade in the Shenandoah Valley, 1864*, Free Press Association, Burlington, Vermont, 1869

Wheelan, Joseph, *Terrible Swift Sword: The Life of Philip H. Sheridan*, Da Capo Press, Philadelphia, Pennsylvania, 2012

INDEX